DATE DUE

AUG 1 5 1985	
SEP - 5 1985	
~~SEP 2 6 1985~~	
MAY 1 8 1987	
NOV 3 0 1987	
NOV 3 0 1987	
FEB 1 6 1988	
JUL 1 1 1988	
AUG 2 1988	
NOV 1 1988	
APR 2 4 1989	
OCT - 9 1990	
DEC 1 7 1990	
DEC 2 1991	
MAY 1 5 1993	
11·27·96	

BRODART, INC.   Cat. No. 23-221

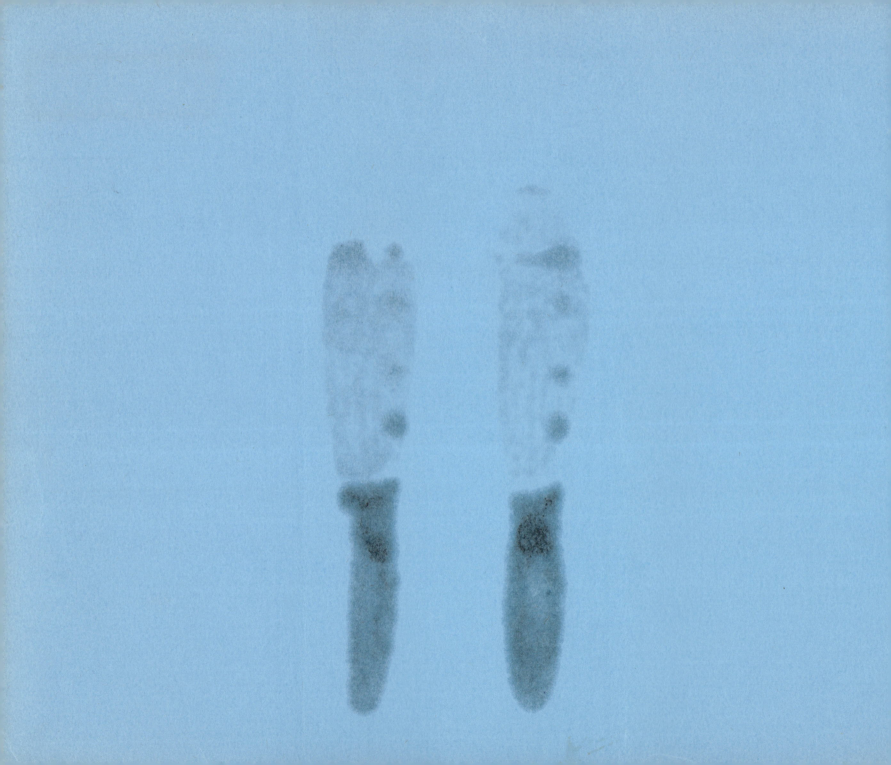

The Jewelry in Your Life

The

Jewelry

in

Your Life

MORTON R. SARETT

Nelson-Hall nh Chicago

Library of Congress Cataloging in Publication Data

Sarett, Morton R
    The jewelry in your life.

    Includes index.
    1. Jewelry.   I. Title.
NK7304.S27   739.27   78.5900
ISBN 0-88229-367-2

Manufactured in the United States of America

10 9 8 7 6 5 4 3 2 1

Contents

Introduction

*J*ewelry plays a dramatic role in the lives of all of us, for it is with jewelry that we usually memorialize our birthdays, graduations, engagements, weddings, anniversaries, holidays—indeed, all the milestones that we share with our loved ones.

Jewelry is with a person all his or her life. The moment a baby is born and takes its first breath, a tiny identification bracelet is placed around its wrist—the very first jewelry in the child's life. Each anniversary of this day is a birthday to be celebrated by family and friends, often with gifts of jewelry that convey their love and sentiment. When the child grows up and graduates from high school and college, he receives still more gifts—often jewelry—from those who rejoice in his accomplishments. And when love is solemnized by engagement and marriage, these occasions are further formalized by gifts of precious stones and metals. Other special days, such as Mother's Day, Father's Day, and Christmas, are made even more memorable by gifts of jewelry that will be cherished for years.

Through the ages jewelry has remained a symbol of rank, power, prestige, and distinction. Jewels have represented authority, religious or temporal, and have adorned crowns and scepters that symbolize their owners' power of life and death over their subjects. Gold, silver, and precious stones have played an important role in the spheres of religion and art and have increased the mystique and allure of kings and queens, movie and television personalities, and men and women from every walk of life.

Jewelry has an appeal of its own. It can mean anything from "I'm thinking of you" to "I love you truly." Jewelry can symbolize a way of life; it can be a signature or a fashion accent. Jewelry can live forever as heirlooms.

Even though jewelry plays so important a part in our lives, most of us know very little about it and have only a vague idea of the differences among the various gems and metals we buy and wear. This book is intended to give as many basic facts about jewelry as possible, including historical background and anecdotes. It cannot, of course, transform anyone into an expert in the field, but it can give you an idea of the kinds of questions to ask when purchasing jewels and give you an appreciation of what makes jewels valuable. Perhaps the best advice we can give the reader is to get to know his or her jeweler. A jeweler of character whose reputation is firmly established in the community will gladly help you learn even more about the jewelry in your life.

The Mystique of Gems & Jewelry

The origins of jewelry are lost in the mists of time. One might imagine that a prehistoric woman, attracted by the beauty of a shining pebble, hung it around her neck, or that an early hunter wore a tooth on a thong to proclaim his success and ability. Whatever its origin, jewelry has been admired, loved, and fought over for centuries. The earliest wearers of beautiful stones probably cared nothing about their value; to them, such jewelry was simply attractive and symbolized something of importance.

The word *jewelry* can be traced to an old French word connoting joy and gladness, and certainly through the centuries gems and jewelry have gladdened many hearts. Gems and jewelry speak a universal language that royalty and common man alike have understood and appreciated.

The earliest ornaments were pebbles, shells, berries, and feathers that were worn as necklaces. Pieces of horn and animal teeth were worn as well, for both their decorative appeal and the magical powers attributed to them. Even before man could read or write, he wore jewelry to decorate himself and to protect his person from a clap of thunder, an enemy, an evil spirit, or a disease or affliction. When he wore, for example, a red stone that coincidentally accomplished one or more of these objectives, it was not unreasonable for him to attribute his good fortune to the power of that stone. If the stone was attractive as well and called attention to the wearer, so much the better.

The origin of the ring, a circle without beginning or end, has been attributed to the knot, symbolizing the magical or binding qualities of something twisted around the finger. Various forms of what we know as the brooch were originally used to pin together skins that were worn for protection from the elements. In the beginning the "pin" may have been a bone or a large thorn with its head engraved with lines, dots, or circles; in time, ivory, wood, and such metals as bronze and gold were used. The first bracelets were worn by men as well as women, not only on the wrist but also on the upper and lower arm. Bangles worn on the ankles called even more attention to their wearer's presence.

Certain colored stones became highly valued for particular purposes. What, for example, could cope with a wound or an affliction of the blood more effectively than a red-colored stone? Hence, it was believed that the garnet, the ruby, the

1

bloodstone—all the color of blood itself—stopped the flow of blood and guarded the bearer against injury. Similar powers were attributed to stones of other colors. Agate, for example, was said to reduce fever and to cure diseases of the eye as well. Sapphire corrected poor vision and assured health, wealth, and strength. Emerald conquered still more eye afflictions and burned in the presence of poison to warn its owner.

Jade was beneficial to the kidneys. Amethyst banished toothache and headache and prevented the bearer from getting drunk. Carnelian tightened loose teeth. Opals strengthened vision and guarded the life and color of blond hair. The diamond could cure leprosy, insanity, and nightmares and guard against poison, witchcraft, and madness. It was also a symbol of the sun and innocence.

Many of these superstitions about gems had their origins in myths and legends, although some were based on truth. Opals, for instance, were originally thought to bring good luck. Early gem setters, however, did not know how to handle them and often broke the stones while attempting to cut them. They then spread the word that opals were unlucky. In 1829 Sir Walter Scott in his novel *Anne of Geierstein* told of Lady Hermione, who wore an enchanted opal in her hair. The gem gave off fiery red flashes when she was angry but sparkled brilliantly when she was happy. One day she became ill and was confined to bed; the next morning all that was left of her was a heap of ashes. The opal she wore was blamed for the misfortune.

Other superstitions about precious stones were based on fear; their owners had no means of protecting their valuables except to circulate stories that the gems they owned brought misfortune, in the hope that a thief would think twice before stealing them. The creation of such fantasies, which in time became legends about the bad luck inherent in certain stones, was perhaps the best safeguard against theft. Many ill-luck stories are replete with details, and persons even today ascribe special powers to certain pieces of jewelry. The copper bracelet, for example, is worn by a great number of modern men and women who sincerely believe that it will protect them from certain ailments.

In addition to such supposed medicinal and other powers, stones also had religious significance. About 5000 B.C. and perhaps earlier, the Babylonians, Egyptians, and Greeks cut into the surfaces of stones to create unique intaglios. Their designs represented their divinities and objects of traditional or religious beliefs. Engraved cylinders were pierced and worn suspended from a cord about the neck or wrist. Eventually there developed from these cylinders personal signets that symbolized authority. Some seals bore deities or animals of combat; others were more personal. The seal of a doctor, for example, might carry his name and the scalpel and lancet of his profession. Deeds of sale were marked by the seal of the seller—a practice that persists to this day in such legal documents. Marriage contracts required the seals of both parties, and debts were acknowledged by the debtor's seal. These seals came into being long before the existence of widespread literacy, and they conveyed orders and instructions of all kinds.

From seals such as these evolved the signet rings of the Middle Ages, engraved with either the emblem or the portrait of the owner. Since the emblem or portrait could be stamped on a piece of softened wax to identify the ring's owner, merchants found these rings especially useful in marking goods to indicate its origin.

It was natural that man should choose precious stones to ornament the objects that were most revered in religious worship. Our present birthstones are derived from the twelve stones in the breastplate of Aaron, the high priest, on which were engraved the names of the twelve tribes of Israel (Exodus 28:17–21). The stones were also said to represent the twelve months of the year, the twelve signs of the zodiac, the twelve apostles, and the twelve foundation stones of the new temple at Jerusalem.

The Bible contains countless references to gems and jewelry. *Sapphire* relates to the Hebrew word *sappir* and denotes a stone that bears an engraving or inscription. The Ten Commandments, the Hebrews believed, were inscribed on sapphire stones; indeed, according to Exodus 24: 9-10, Moses and his companions saw "the God of Israel: and there was under his feet as it were a paved work of a sapphire stone . . ."

The offerings by the children of Israel in the wilderness for decorating the tabernacle and forming the golden calf were thusly described: "The men and women brought bracelets and earrings and rings and tablets, all jewels of gold," and the golden calf was made up of "gifts of earrings by men and women." In Proverbs 31:10, we read: "Who can find a virtuous woman? for her price is far above rubies." Isaiah tells of the daughters of Zion wearing "metal anklets making a tinkling about their feet." And in Isaiah 61:10 we find: ". . . my soul shall be joyful in my God; for he hath clothed me with the garments of salvation, he hath covered me with the robe of righteousness, as a bridegroom decketh himself with ornaments, and as a bride adorneth herself with her jewels."

The earliest known naturalist was Theophrastus (372?-287? B.C.), a brilliant disciple of Aristotle. He described the gemstones known in his time and classified them so well that his findings were the rule until the end of the eighteenth century. He explained and discussed such gemological principles as fracture, color, transparency, luster, hardness, weight, and fusibility. Many of his conclusions proved to be remarkably accurate. He revealed, for instance, that pearl was a product of the inedible oyster, that coral was a stonelike growth in the sea, and that amber was a resin from the trees of the pine family.

The science of gemology grew from this beginning, and man began to study minerals scientifically to ascertain their individual qualities. Probably the greatest gem expert of his era was Pliny the Elder (23-79 A.D.), the Roman scholar who bequeathed to us the foundation of mineralogy in his famous encyclopedia, *Natural History*. He set up the first test to distinguish precious stones from glass imitations by noting the differences in their weights. Pliny also revealed that the appearance and value of stones could be improved by heating them in honey. The best way to detect a false stone, he pointed out, was to break off a fragment and determine its hardness, a procedure that some Roman jewelers refused to follow. More than two thousand years ago, Pliny recognized that hardness was one of the best gemological tests.

According to Pliny, the use of precious stones as jewelry began on the rocks of the Caucasus, where Prometheus was bound. Prometheus, he said, put a small piece of the rock to which he was chained in a bit of iron and placed it on his finger. Thus, he had not only a ring but a gem-set one.

Pliny warned that turquoise would lose its color when in contact with oils, wine, or perspiration, and he showed how to stain agate. He revealed also that the brilliancy of garnets would be considerably enhanced if they were steeped in honey for fourteen days, an effect that would last a similar number of months. Pliny did not use the adjective "precious" but instead classified gemstones into two groups—the "more noble gems" and "those of inferior quality."

Although he actually saw only a few diamonds, which had come from India, Pliny was amazed at their hardness and described them as "wonderful and unnatural." Even then, diamond splinters were used to cut the hardest gems known.

It is believed that gold was discovered during the sixth millennium B.C. in the form of nuggets carried by rivers and streams, but it was too soft to make the kinds of tools Neolithic man needed to survive. The first gold miners were the Egyptians, who looked upon gold as solidified fire, like the sun; indeed, the precious metal became the symbol of Ra, their sun god and divinity. A similar connection between the sun and gold was made by the Incas of Peru.

Gold has been used for thousands of years to make precious jewels, ornaments, coins, and many other objects used for religious or secular purposes. Even treasures that have remained buried for centuries emerge as beautiful and shiny when unearthed as they were on the day they were created. Gold can be melted down and used over and over again. Gold can never be destroyed. It is eternal in its fascination, beauty, and use. A piece of jewelry fashioned today may well contain gold from the temple of Solomon or from an Egyptian tomb.

Beautiful jewelry was the fashion as long ago as four thousand years, and the people then wore rings, earrings, bracelets, and brooches much as we do today. The Egyptians made theirs of silver, enamel, and imitation and natural stones. To the Greeks, the beauty of a piece of jewelry was as important as the value of the materials used to make it. Ingeniously, they worked fine threads of gold into butterfly or grasshopper shapes. The Greeks showed a fondness for cameos and for jasper, amber, and coral.

The Etruscans of northern Italy created magnificent jewelry having intricate patterns with great skill. The surface of their gold jewelry was shiny instead of grainy and looked as if fine gold powder had been evenly sprinkled over it. The Romans, on the other hand, wore elaborate jewelry to show off their wealth, and Roman politicians adorned their fingers with bejeweled rings in order to impress those about them with their importance and high standing. Julius Caesar was an enthusiastic collector of gems, and at a wedding party, the wife of the Emperor Caligula attracted considerable attention and envy by wearing superb emeralds and pearls. The women of

Rome, like the men, wore many rings, often on all their fingers.

When the Roman Empire split in 395 A.D., its eastern portion, the Byzantine Empire, became the most powerful state of the Mediterranean area. Constantinople, its capital, replaced Rome as the center of art and fashion. The jewelry styles of this ancient city influenced the entire Western world. Byzantine designs featured symbols and formal patterns, and pieces of gold were enameled in bright reds and blues. The wealthy wore ropes of pearls and emeralds, and sometimes their clothing was so encrusted with jewels that it was difficult for them to move about.

During the Middle Ages, most jewelry craftsmen were monks who devoted their efforts to making religious decorations. Most of the precious gems they used were part of the loot that the Crusaders had brought back from the Holy Land. Jewelers' guilds began sometime after the ninth century, and by 1327 the goldsmiths in London were recognized as a major craft group and had formed their own association.

One unusual type of jewelry that originated during the Middle Ages was the pomander. This openwork metal ball containing perfume was a useful article in those days when city smells were often unpleasant.

The people of the Renaissance also took great interest in jewelry. New methods were developing, and in the fifteenth century gem-cutters learned how to cut a diamond to give it greater brilliance and bring out its fire. The jewelry of this period was very colorful, and one piece might combine different stones and enamels. In addition, pearls were often used. King Henry VIII was said to be such an avid collector of jewelry that he amassed in his lifetime 234 rings and 324 brooches. The wealthy wore as many as three rings on each finger.

Before the sixteenth century, men adorned themselves

with as much jewelry as women did and sometimes more. When women began to wear more jewelry than men, however, many new designs appeared, a great number of them inspired by butterflies, frogs, bugs, flowers, trumpets, and even mousetraps.

The most popular form of jewelry was the delicately fashioned pendant, often decorated with a religious or mythological scene. The girdle—a flexible belt worn over outer clothing and on which small pieces of jewelry were hung—was almost equally favored.

After the reign of Queen Elizabeth I of England (1533–1603) women wore somewhat less jewelry than before. Men, however, still displayed flashing gems of all kinds, especially on their hats. More delicate jewelry was coming into fashion, and throughout Europe old, bulky pieces were melted down and remodeled into the newer styles.

Nevertheless, the imperial crown that Catherine the Great of Russia ordered for her coronation in 1762 was so ornate that it could not be completed in time for the ceremony. The exterior of this magnificent creation contained 4,936 diamonds of varied sizes weighing 2,858 carats, and the central ridge was embellished by matched pearls weighing 763 carats. The pure white Orloff diamond of 189.6 carats, which was valued then at more than a million dollars, was set in the head of the imperial scepter.

Around 1804, the year Napoleon I became ruler of France, Greek and Roman fashions enjoyed a new wave of popularity. Now men wore less jewelry than women. The women, on the other hand, wore jeweled rings on their toes, and cameos became popular because the Empress Josephine was fond of them.

This renaissance of Greek and Roman jewelry styles was of short duration. When Queen Victoria took the English throne in 1837, the styles began to change again. The Vic-

Scottish enamelled gold and jewelled necklace. Second half of 16th century contemporaneous with Mary Queen of Scots, very rare and of exceptional quality. An inscription written in Scottish dialect reads, "Hope feedeth me."

torian jewelry that came into vogue was often decorated with tiny figures of knights in shining armor and elegant ladies. Now sentiment played the greatest part in the design and wearing of jewelry.

Late in the nineteenth century, French designers began to create jewelry of outstanding beauty and delicacy. René Lalique (1860–1945), the greatest of these designers, used stones for their beauty rather than for their intrinsic value. Lalique became famous as an artist-jeweler for exquisite and unusual styles in which he combined a great variety of stones. Lalique was a glassmaker as well, and his fine glass objects in distinctive colors and designs were equally in demand.

One of the most talented of all jewelry creators was Peter Carl Fabergé, jeweler for the Russian court, whose best-known works are the jeweled eggs presented by the czars to the czarinas on Easter. The first of these was made in 1884 and was followed by many others—all displayed at the World Exposition in Paris in 1900 to great acclaim. Fabergé used different shades of gold and blended them with the colors of enamels and gems. Enamels particularly were his specialty, and he made them in a variety of colors and finishes to further enhance the design. Fabergé's skill was so extraordinary that he could copy a rare historic treasure so skillfully that his work was virtually indistinguishable from the original.

Perhaps the most beautiful and famous of all the Fabergé eggs was made in 1906 for Czar Nicholar II of Russia to give to his wife, Alexandra Feodirovna. Its outer shell is made of a pale purple enamel decorated with diamond ribbons and bows, and one large diamond is set on its pointed end. Inside the egg are gold water lilies and, on a blue aquamarine, a swan that moves gracefully and automatically when wound up under one wing.

Many other pieces of jewelry have their own special stories. The most famous of all religious rings is the Fisherman's Ring, the gold seal ring of the pope, which shows St. Peter in a boat, fishing. The name of the reigning pope is inscribed around the ring, and when he dies, the ring is either broken in half or buried with him and a new one made for his successor.

One of the most celebrated necklaces in history was the diamond necklace that helped bring about the French Revolution. Louis XV had ordered this fabulously expensive necklace for his mistress Madame du Barry but died of smallpox before the jewelers had finished it. The jewelers tried to sell the necklace to the new king, Louis XVI, to give to Marie Antoinette, but he could not afford it. The necklace, which disappeared, nevertheless became a symbol of the royal family's extravagance at a time when many of their subjects were starving.

A large and exceptionally beautiful opal ring was the subject of a story about a Roman senator named Nonius. Mark Antony saw the opal and wanted to give it to Cleopatra. Mark Antony gave Nonius the choice of selling him the precious opal or being banished, believing that the senator would not leave Rome. Nonius chose to leave Rome with his ring.

In America jewelry-making is one of the oldest trades, for it was practiced by the Indians many years before the first Europeans landed. The Dutch and the English brought buckles, brooches, and rings with them, and one's personal attire was incomplete without such ornamentation. As a result, gold- and silversmithing were two of our first industries. Smiths made jewelry of all kinds as well as trinkets for the Indians, medals, and snuffboxes. Silver boxes lined with gold, containing parchments conferring the "freedom of the city," were presented to distinguished guests. The people of New York presented Alexander Hamilton with a gold box studded with precious stones after his stirring defense of the liberties of the press in 1784, and similar boxes were given to Lafayette,

Washington, and other patriots. So prominent were the goldsmiths and jewelers of the day that some thirty-five of them appeared in the procession that celebrated the adoption of the new Constitution in Philadelphia in 1788.

Paul Revere, in addition to his distinction as a patriot, was a trained goldsmith and silversmith who practiced his craft in Boston. The Revere bowl is still a popular product of today's silversmiths.

Jewelry at this time had still another purpose. People accumulated it as a means of saving their money, for until the nineteenth century few banks existed. Money that was made into articles of gold and silver could be identified easily if the items were specially designed and marked. Furthermore, jewels were not as likely to be stolen as coins might be. Unlike present coins, early ones were almost pure silver or gold. A customer gave the jeweler the coins needed to make the article of jewelry he wanted, and the coins were melted down and reformed. The jeweler, therefore, had to be a man people would trust as they would a banker.

Gems and jewelry are so highly regarded that many of their names have become synonyms for beauty. When we describe someone or something as a gem or a jewel, we mean the ultimate in quality and perfection. Our literature contains allusions to ruby lips, pearly teeth, sapphire eyes, coral ears, jet hair, turquoise skies, emerald meadows, and silver or golden hair. These images reflect the universal appeal of gems and jewels and show that it is as real today as it was thousands of years ago. In a world of constant change, gems and jewelry remain eternally valued. As lasting symbols of love and affection and as gifts for memorable occasions, they have a romance and a mystique that will probably live forever.

Fashions in Jewelry through the Ages

The most renowned collectors of gems and jewelry have always been royalty—kings, queens, and emperors whose power and phenomenal wealth made it possible for them to own and wear bejeweled crowns, tiaras, and coronets, and indeed, any kind of gem or jewel they desired. The cliche about someone or something's being worth a king's ransom is no doubt derived from the incalculable value of the royal gem and jewelry collections a monarch could fall back on if he found himself in a dire emergency.

Queen Cleopatra, whose charms and beauty are legendary, had a great passion for gems of every kind. Fortunately, she owned a large emerald mine in Egypt and could indulge her fondness for these stones. Not only did she herself wear emeralds in abundance, but she is said to have given them to favorite ambassadors as personal mementos. Cleopatra loved pearls, too, and when she gave her celebrated banquet for Mark Antony, she wore a pair of magnificent pearl earrings of incalculable value. At that same feast she is supposed to have dissolved one of her pearls in a goblet of wine and drunk it

down to demonstrate to Mark Antony her wealth and power. To do this, the pearl would have to be pulverized and the wine turned to vinegar. Although it is unlikely that this actually happened, there is little doubt that Cleopatra did indeed impress him and that she set trends in jewelry as well as in affairs of the heart.

Hardly a king or queen has lacked a hoard of gems and jewelry, for the possession of jewels gives enormous prestige and sways friend and foe alike. Some rulers murdered, plundered, and intrigued to build up their caches. Perhaps their subjects, who had to foot the bills, were expected to feel a sense of pride in the fabulous possessions of their rulers even though they knew that the jewelry would never benefit them. As far as we know, the most benevolent use of such jewels by a reigning monarch was made by Queen Isabella of Spain when she pledged hers to help finance Christopher Columbus on his voyage to the New World.

Kings and queens enjoyed wearing as well as hoarding their gems and occasionally set new styles. Henry III, for example, was the envy of French courtiers for his elegant earrings, and Louis XIV created quite a stir when he sported a garment decorated with thousands of diamonds.

While royalty flaunted their jewelry, so did their mistresses. In 1760 Louis XV of France boasted not one mistress but two—Madame de Pompadour and the aforementioned Madame du Barry, each of whom loved luxury, had considerable influence, and set the fashion pace of their era. Madame de Pompadour is credited with somewhat better taste than her successor and was known for her elegant jewelry creations and cameos. Madame du Barry, however, craved all the jewelry she could get and bought from nearly every jeweler she saw. When a large part of her costly collection of diamonds, pearls, emeralds, and other gems was stolen, she was distraught and tried to recover them. But, as we know, the people were suffering from widespread poverty at the time. So angered were they over her extravagance, including the gems that had been bought at their expense, that they ultimately led her to the guillotine.

A far more fortunate French mistress of an earlier time was Agnes Sorel, the gay, saucy companion of Charles VII. Always extremely fond of jewelry and what it did for her appearance and status, she asked the court jeweler to make her something unique for an upcoming court ball. With diamonds she gave him he created a spectacular necklace for the occasion. Until that time (1437), no woman except royalty had ever dared to wear diamonds in public; they had been worn primarily by men of noble rank. When mistress Sorel made her grand entrance at the ball, the effect of her diamonds was exactly what she had calculated. All eyes, including those of Charles VII, were drawn to her dazzling presence. Agnes Sorel was a sensation, and it became a firmly established fashion for women to wear diamonds on every stylish occasion.

The European courts with their pomp and ceremony were a perfect setting for jewels of every kind. Candles provided the light for evening festivities, and gems picked up candlelight perfectly. Diamonds became increasingly popular, and jewelers learned to set them in such a way as to bring out their maximum brilliance.

Marie Antoinette's diamond necklace leaves little doubt that diamonds were indeed her best friends. The necklace consisted of 647 diamonds weighing a total of 2,842 carats and was made in two sections: a choker with festoons, and a large garland for the bodice that tied at the back of the neck with ribbons. To duplicate such a necklace today would cost many millions of dollars. The necklace was divided and in 1785 brought to England, where it was sold and the twenty-two largest diamonds incorporated into another necklace.

Although facets had been cut on diamonds for many centuries, in 1475 a talented Belgian lapidary named Louis de Berquem of Bruges was the first to discover how to cut them symmetrically. De Berquem is regarded as the father of modern diamond-cutting, and portraits of him are still displayed in diamond-cutting centers throughout the world. In the late seventeenth century, a Venetian named Vincenzo Peruzzi developed the "brilliant cut," which shaped a diamond so it would capture and reflect the light on many facets and appear even more brilliant than before.

As the wearing of jewelry became more important for women than for men, it also became customary to own large sets of jewels. A full set consisted of a large, dramatic necklace, a small necklace, a brooch, large and small earrings, rings, a corsage brooch, some bracelets, and possibly a tiara. A more modest set included a necklace, earrings, rings, a brooch, and a pair of bracelets—the basic minimum for the well-dressed woman of the times. It is interesting that even today certain

European churches lend a bride a complete set of jewelry on her wedding day to make her look more attractive than anyone else present.

As fashions in jewelry changed, which they did continually, stones were often reset to create new, stylish pieces. This meant, of course, that one had to pay only for the labor that went into making the new jewelry.

Among the fashions in jewelry for men in the eighteenth century were shoe buckles, which continued to grow in size until they covered nearly the entire instep. At a glance one could determine social standing: a diamond buckle was the mark of a courtier; a rich farmer wore silver buckles to church on Sundays and gilt ones during the week; a rakish squire preferred polished steel with imitation stones; and any person of high fashion might wear buckles with glass ornaments.

We have mentioned before that classic jewelry became popular in Napoleon's day. He himself was such an afficionado that he founded a special school to teach handicapped students to cut and polish stones and work with metals. To insure an adequate supply of proper materials, he ordered his generals to take them from the fine collections of affluent Romans.

After Napolean had crowned himself emperor, he began wearing diamonds at all court functions and soon the gems were seen in aigrettes, combs, and tiaras. Josephine had an even more insatiable lust for jewelry, and she helped herself to the crown jewels that Napolean had generously provided for her and squandered huge amounts on new acquisitions, including a great many of the cameos that she adored and coveted. Napoleon's crown was a simple band adorned with cameos, no doubt inspired by Josephine's taste.

At Napoleon's coronation the pope touched off a new fashion by presenting rosaries to the ladies of the court.

Napoleon himself set another trend when he gave his sister a bracelet embellished with stones to celebrate the birth of her daughter. The initials of the stones spelled out the name of the child, and in no time such motto bracelets became very popular.

When Josephine and Napoleon parted, she naturally took all her jewelry with her, and when he later married Marie Louise of Austria, he was distressed that his new wife had no jewelry wardrobe whatsoever. He quickly remedied this by giving her a fabulous collection of ornate pieces replete with spectacular diamonds, pearls, emeralds, rubies, and opals. He further indulged himself with diamonds of every size. One of the most famous was the 140.5-carat Regent diamond, which had been found in India and had previously rested in the crowns of Louis XV and XVI. It now embellished Napoleon's sword.

As time went on, diamonds became more and more valued and were worn in rivières or necklaces, matched or graduated, with a large center stone. A diamond of ten carats was considered a fair size, but many sought larger ones of at least fifteen carats and preferably forty. The large solitaire zoomed to popularity for rings, pins, and pendants.

When Louis Napoleon, Napoleon I's nephew, married Eugénie in 1853, he had the crown jewels set into many new forms of jewelry to her liking. Gala balls and public functions gave her an opportunity to show off her sumptuous and valuable jewels, and she made the most of these opportunities. Eugénie had a special attachment to diamonds and pearls, and it was she who popularized the string of pearls for evening wear. Under her fashion leadership, diamonds and colored stones were made into dazzling necklaces, bracelets, earrings, and pins. Large pins, often in naturalistic designs such as large flowers, were very much in vogue. The deep decolletages of the times were heaven-sent for jewelers, and they took full advantage of this fashion to create incredibly elaborate and eye-catching necklaces and jewels.

Many royal figures have played a role in spotlighting gems and jewels and attracting attention as well as envy to themselves, but it was not until diamonds were discovered in South Africa that they became almost universally worn. Diamonds ceased to be the special privilege of royalty and those of noble birth. After 1870 or so, diamonds could be owned and worn by people of every class—and they were.

Fashions in jewelry have changed with each passing generation, with the tastes of every period in history. A king, queen, courtesan, dictator, patron, or celebrity can always influence fashions momentarily, but the real strength of gems and jewelry lies in their everlasting beauty, whether displayed in a museum or in a jewelry store or on the hand, ears, or throat of a woman.

An important English pendant locket with a cameo of Queen Elizabeth I. It would probably have been given by the Queen to one of her noblemen or an admiral. She was known to have said that no dog in her court would wear anyone else's collar, so she gave decorations that had been commissioned on her own.

ᵗʰᵉDiamond: King of Gems

Twinkle, twinkle, little star,
How I wonder what you are,
Up above the world so high,
Like a diamond in the sky.

Our image of the diamond begins in early childhood with nursery rhymes and fairy tales and grows through the years. Around the world the diamond is the unchallenged king of gems.

Diamond is the hardest substance known. The word itself is derived from the Latin *adamas*, which means "firm," "unyielding," "durable." History and tradition have proved that the diamond is indeed the most enduring of all gems.

Chemically, the diamond is pure carbon, a common element found in coal, graphite, soot, and lampblack. The diamond differs, however, in that it is crystalline carbon, formed deep in the earth many millions of years ago through tremendous volcanic heat and pressure. When molten lava cooled, it formed the basic igneous rock that is the source of diamonds.

DIAMOND MINING

Diamonds were first found about 800 B.C. along the Kistna and Godavari Rivers in India; the best ones came from the Golconda area. From there, traders transported them to Rome and Greece and east to China. Millions of carats worth of diamonds were discovered in the gravel beds along these rivers. The largest diamonds became the property of Indian royalty and were immortalized in such famous gems as the Koh-i-noor, the Orloff, and the Great Mogul. Many other huge stones of like origin and ownership disappeared and were doubtless stolen.

In the middle of the seventeenth century Jean Baptiste Tavernier, the great French traveler and jeweler—the Marco Polo of the gem world—returned from his voyage to India with tales of fabulous Indian diamonds. Each had a colorful and violent history of its own. In 1642 Tavernier himself brought back a huge blue diamond that he sold in 1668 to Louis XIV of France. It was among the French crown jewels stolen during

13

the French Revolution, and is believed to have turned up later to become the famed Hope diamond. The Orloff, which was supposedly taken from an idol's eye in a temple in southern India, and which later became part of the Russian crown jewels, is thought by some to have been part of the Great Mogul, the largest known Indian diamond, missing for many years. Other notable diamonds—the Koh-i-noor, for example —are now among the British crown jewels, and the Regent is in the Louvre.

In 1726 prospectors searching for gold in Brazil picked up some pretty pebbles in the streams they were panning and put them to use as gambling chips or markers. To their surprise and delight, the pretty pebbles proved to be genuine diamonds. There followed such a diamond rush to Tejuco, the town where the discovery was made, that it was quickly renamed Diamantina. The South American diamond industry reached a whopping sixteen million carats per year, and until the middle of the nineteenth century South America was an important source of supply.

The most dramatic and historic diamond discovery took place in 1866. While playing on the banks of the Orange River near his home in Capetown, South Africa, a young boy picked up a bright and unusual pebble and brought it home. His mother thought little of his find, and when a neighbor took a fancy to it and offered to buy it, she gave it to him for nothing. He took the pebble to a trader, Jack O'Reilly, who bought it for a small amount in the hope that it might have some use. When O'Reilly found that he could write on a windowpane with the pebble, he knew he had something unusual and took the stone to a mineralogist, who made some tests and told him that the pebble was a genuine diamond.

The diamond weighed twenty-one carats, and O'Reilly sold it to the governor of the Cape Colony for $2,500. First it was called the O'Reilly; then later it was renamed the Eureka, which in Greek means "I have found it!" The Eureka was ex-

hibited in Paris and soon the whole world was buzzing with the news—"Diamonds in South Africa!" This discovery triggered an enormous diamond rush. By 1880 there were ten thousand diggers in Kimberley alone, and the mine there had become the largest man-made crater in the world, 3,106 feet deep and known as the "Big Hole."

The birth of South African diamond mining was long and difficult, marked as it was by the violence of tribal wars, thievery, squatters'-rights disputes, smuggling, and black marketing. Men of all ages, from all walks of life, from all nations came to search for diamonds. The early adventurers, though, had little success until 1869, when a large diamond was discovered farther south. This diamond, later named the Star of South Africa, spurred the diggers further, and the hunt spread.

The first miners confined their search to rivers and the gravels surrounding them. But the rivers were only carriers, and soon diamonds were traced to deposits of "yellow ground." These deposits could be worked to great depths, but the miners usually stopped when they reached the hard "blue ground" underneath. In 1876 someone thought up the "volcanic pipe" theory, which suggested that diamonds reached the earth's surface through escape pipes in the ground as a result of the immense heat and pressures of underground volcanos. A variation of this idea was the belief that the pipe is a root of an old volcano that once rose above the surface of the earth and was gradually leveled off to the flat South African veldt.

In addition to gravel, alluvial-deposit, and blue-ground mining, modern methods have extended to exploring the seas in the hope that diamonds may have been left there after volcanic eruptions in the waters in ages past or have been carried there from inland by rivers.

Even in the richest blue-ground areas, gem diamonds are rare, and mining them requires enormous efforts. It is estimated that only one part in 35 million by weight of blue ground is diamond and that about 250 tons of ore must be mined and crushed to yield a single carat of gem-quality diamond. Of all the diamonds found, only about 20 percent are of gem quality and can be used for jewelry. The remainder, used as industrial diamonds, are dull and unattractive to the eye but are in great demand. Industrial diamonds are used for operations requiring the utmost in hardness—they are found in food-processing machinery, record-making and related equipment, surgical instruments, and, of course, in tools to cut other diamonds. Hardness tests show that a diamond is up to 150 times as hard as corundum, which ranks second to diamond on the Mohs' scale of hardness.

In addition to being hard, the diamond has exceptionally high dispersion, or "fire." When white light or sunlight is passed through a prism or facets of a stone, it is resolved into its component colors—from the red through the violet shades of the spectrum. The width of the spectrum (the distance between the red and the violet) varies for each kind of stone. The diamond's exceptionally wide spectrum and high dispersion account for its enormous "fire."

The discovery of diamonds in South Africa created the new mass market for diamonds as opposed to the "class" market that had existed until that time. No longer were diamonds the prerogative of royalty, nobility, and the very rich. Today diamonds are available at popular prices, and about three of every four brides in the United States receive a diamond engagement ring.

DIAMOND CUTTING

A newly mined diamond can scarcely be recognized for what it is. Dull, greasy, without any symmetry of design, it hardly looks like a potential jewel. The transformation of the homely "diamond in the rough" into a gem requires skilled craftsmanship, effort, and patience, and the slightest error can be costly. The craft of diamond-cutting requires many years of apprenticeship and experience and is traditionally passed down from father to son. The diamond-cutter must eliminate flaws and create the desired shape, yet still retain as much weight as possible. In the process, the diamond is likely to lose more than half its weight.

First the diamond is closely examined for flaws and for its structural grain. A large, valuable stone may be studied for many months before the cutter proceeds. Usually the diamond is first sawed in two. A few are cleaved, notably the larger gems. A cutter cleaves a diamond by scratching a rather small groove along the line of the grain. He sets a steel rule along the groove and taps the back of the rule lightly. This is sufficient to split the gem in two. If the stone has been marked in precisely the right place and the force is just right, the diamond will cleave along its grain; if not, the gem may shatter and thousands of dollars will be lost in a fraction of a second.

The famous Cullinan diamond, weighing 3,601 carats (about a pound and a third), presented a classic challenge to the diamond-cutter. It was the biggest gem diamond ever found. Joseph Asscher, a famous Amsterdam diamond-cutter, was chosen for the nerve-racking task. After months of study, he decided on his line of cleavage. This in itself requires an intuitive genius: the grain that the line of cleavage must follow is invisible.

Asscher drew a V-shaped groove along the line. As he tensely approached the world's biggest diamond, the mallet in his hand shook and he broke into a nervous sweat. When he raised his mallet, not even the sound of breathing could be heard in the room. He dropped the mallet down against the steel rule, and the steel rule broke in half! But, miraculously, the Cullinan remained intact.

Asscher went to a hospital to recuperate from his ordeal. When he felt strong enough to try the stone again, he had his personal physician accompany him. Once again Asscher

STEPS IN CUTTING A DIAMOND

The rough diamond may be shown in a diagram as an octahedron.

The octahedron is sawed in two, a little above its middle.

After rounding or girdling the diamond looks like this. The flat top is its table; the circumference is its girdle.

Here the diamond has four main facets above the girdle (two in front and two behind) and four main facets below the girdle.

The stone now has eight facets above the girdle and eight more below it. This is like the 17-facet "single cut" diamond.

The brillianteerer has here cut additional facets on the stone, approaching the fully cut diamond with 58 facets.

struck the steel rule with his malllet. This time the Cullinan cleaved cleanly in two, exactly along the line Asscher had chosen. Asscher did not know that he had been successful until sometime later, for he had fainted when the mallet struck!

The more usual method of cutting is sawing—a long and laborious process that may take several hours in the case of a one-carat stone. The diamond to be sawed is placed in cup and held firmly by a special cement. The cup itself is on the end of a long metal arm, which is counterweighted so that the downward weight is gradually increased. This weight presses the diamond against a rapidly revolving disc of phosphor bronze. The edge of the disc, which cuts the diamond, is no thicker than a piece of writing paper and is impregnated with a mixture of olive oil and diamond dust.

The weight keeps the diamond pressing against the whirring blade with constant pressure. The cutting edge of the saw is continually renewed as it picks up dust from the part of the diamond it cuts away.

Girdling, the next step in the process, is done by pressing the diamond against another diamond so that it is roughly shaped and given an edge. Each of these steps demands precision craftsmanship, because everything must be done in proportion. An error means the proportions must be changed; the diamond must be cut again, made smaller, and thus reduced in value.

Even at this point there is no sign of the diamond's luster, which must be brought out by polishing or faceting. The diamond is secured in a cup at the end of tongs and held against a rapidly revolving iron plate or scaif resembling a phonograph record. The plate, like the saw, is covered with a mixture of olive oil and diamond dust.

Most diamonds have fifty-eight facets, of which thirty-three are above the girdle (the point of widest circumference) and twenty-five below, including the culet, or flattened bottom point. To yield the maximum dispersion of light or fire, these facets are placed precisely according to a fixed pattern. The diamond must be moved in its holder many times during this process, sometimes at a new angle for each facet.

Expert diamond-cutting naturally adds to a diamond's value and brings out its fullest potential beauty. The value of a diamond is determined by what jewelers call the four *C*'s—color, cut, clarity and carat weight.

Color. The top color diamonds are crystal clear. A diamond reflects the light surrounding it. While a tinge of color may affect value, it will not necessarily detract from the diamond's sparkle. Diamonds are found in many colors—blue, pink, brown, yellow, green, and so on. Some of these are highly valued as "fancies" and are collectors' items. The rarest of all diamond colors is red. Some of the world's famous diamonds are a pronounced color. The Hope, for example, is a deep blue.

The term "blue-white" is sometimes applied to diamonds, but Federal Trade Commission rules state that it cannot be used to describe a diamond that, under normal, north daylight or its equivalent, shows any color or trace of color other than blue or bluish. Few diamonds actually qualify.

Cut. The skill and precision that transform a diamond into a gem are, as mentioned before, important factors in its value. The proportions of the stone and the expert polishing of each facet enhance the diamond's brilliance and beauty.

The most popular shape, the round or brilliant cut, is generally used in rings. Other favorite cuts include the marquise, the emerald, the heart, the oval, and the pear. The marquise, named in honor of the elegant Marquise de Montespan, mistress of Louis XIV, is an elongated ellipse pointed at both ends. The emerald is a rectangle with squared-off diagonal corners. The pear, oval, and heart are what their names imply.

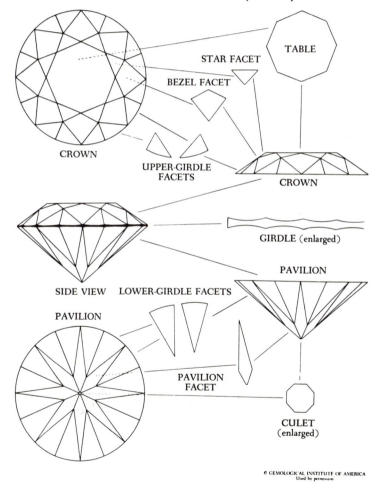

DIAMOND-BRILLIANT CUT (ROUND)

TABLE

STAR FACET

BEZEL FACET

CROWN

UPPER-GIRDLE FACETS

CROWN

GIRDLE (enlarged)

PAVILION

SIDE VIEW   LOWER-GIRDLE FACETS

PAVILION

PAVILION FACET

CULET (enlarged)

© GEMOLOGICAL INSTITUTE OF AMERICA
Used by permission

PROPORTIONS OF DIAMONDS

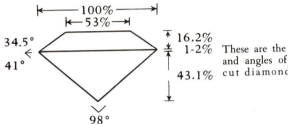

These are the proportions and angles of a properly cut diamond (round).

In a properly cut diamond, light entering through the table and bezel facets is reflected back through the top.

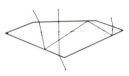

If the stone is cut too shallow, part of the light leaks out the bottom.

If the stone is cut too deep, much of the light leaks out the sides.

(The last two cuts are exaggerated for these diagrams, but a diamond need be only a little too shallow or too deep before it starts to leak light.)

Each cut has a different look that suits the individuality of the diamond and the variety of jewelry designs in which it is used. The following cuts are used for smaller diamonds:

1. *The small full cut* is a brilliant or round cut of a tiny diamond. It has the usual fifty-eight facets despite its small size. Such a diamond may grace the heart of a locket.

2. *The single cut* is a much simpler cut in which the number of facets is reduced to seventeen. Single cut diamonds are small and used for decoration.

3. *The baguette*, a French word meaning *rod*, is a style of step cutting for small, rectangularly-shaped diamonds. Baguette and tapered baguette diamonds are most often used to set off larger gems and to embellish mountings.

4. *Melee*. Small, full, or single cut diamonds grouped together and used to embellish mountings, settings, or larger gems.

5. *Pave.* The setting of many diamonds flush with the surface and very close together so as to expose the least amount of metal. With this method, many small diamonds can create an impressive, glittering show.

Clarity. Since the diamond is a product of nature, it may have a carbon spot or other inclusion or crack in the crystal structure. Again, the smaller and fewer of these, the greater a diamond's value. According to government regulations, a diamond called "perfect" or "flawless" should have no inclusions visible under ten-power magnification.

Carat Weight. The carat is a unit of weight for diamonds. The word comes from the name of the seed of the carob tree, which was historically the unit of measure for diamonds because it was uniform in weight. A carat weighs 200 milligrams, or about .007 ounce, and is divided into one hundred points, as a dollar is divided into cents. A ten-point diamond, for example, weighs one-tenth of a carat; a seventy-five-point diamond weighs three-quarters of a carat.

The larger the diamond, of course, the rarer it is and the more expensive. For instance, other things being equal, a two-carat diamond will cost considerably more than twice as much as a one-carat stone; a three-carat one may cost six or seven times as much.

Diamonds vary considerably in quality. The fact that a diamond does not meet the highest quality standards in every respect does not necessarily detract from its attractiveness. Each diamond has its individual identity and appeal.

DIAMONDS IN FASHION

As recounted in Chapter 2, Agnes Sorel struck a dramatic blow for women's fashion by having her diamonds strung into the world's first diamond necklace. The jeweler who created that daring innovation was a Frenchman named Jacques Coeur.

His inspiration has had far-reaching consequences. Now a simple strand of pearls becomes the epitome of elegance when clasped by a cluster of diamonds, and a plain wristwatch is transformed into a dramatic piece of jewelry with the addition of some diamonds to lend it sparkle. Emeralds, rubies, sapphires, opals, practically all gemstones become more fashionable when combined with diamonds.

Modern jewelry designers are creating new and striking designs for diamonds in every price range. Small diamonds are now used effectively, and illusion settings have been devised to make the smallest diamonds appear larger. Large diamonds are used in multicolored rings, pins, and earrings combining a variety of precious stones and in other unique designs.

The greatest male collector of diamonds was the colorful and portly "Diamond Jim" Brady, who not only wore diamonds day and night but flaunted his collection everywhere. As a traveling salesman of railroad equipment, he had to see his customers face to face and make them respect and trust him.

His fabulous diamonds gained him instant entree to the offices of the powerful railroad magnates of the Gay Nineties and "Diamond Jim" always had something new to show them. His most famous item was his "Transportation Set," composed of various railroad cars and set with a total of 2,548 diamonds. Altogether he amassed some thirty sets with more than twenty thousand diamonds of various sizes and shapes and about six thousand colored stones. To those who criticized him for being ostentatious, he announced: "You fellers can talk all you like about what's done and what ain't. As for me, I've always noticed that them as has 'em wears 'em!"

Brady kept his gems in a vault and each day sent a messenger to pick up what he would wear that day to the races, the theater, or a business meeting. To woo the lovely Lillian Russell, he gave her many gifts of diamonds and most certainly attracted her attention if not her heart.

Few men of the day followed Brady's example of wearing diamonds; most of them felt that the gems should adorn women exclusively. In recent years, however, more and more men have been wearing diamonds in rings, cuff links, tie tacks, studs, wallet clips, watches, and other items, in keeping with the general trend toward male fashion consciousness.

DIAMONDS AND LOVE

No one really knows when diamonds first became the gemstone of love and romance. We do know that ancient Romans used diamonds as a "gem of reconciliation" between angry lovers or quarreling spouses and that engagement and wedding rings date back at least four thousand years. Conceivably some of them had diamonds in them.

The first known diamond engagement ring was given by Archduke Maximilian of Austria to his royal intended, Mary of Burgundy, in 1477. Fortunately for tradition, Maximilian was

Diamonds in the rough. Rough diamonds are transformed into brilliant gems by the process of cutting. Although many diamonds occur in nature as octahedron crystals, they can take a variety of other shapes as is shown here. Whatever the shape of the rough, however, the precise operations of cutting produce a finished diamond that gives the maximum refraction and diffusion of light. For it is the behavior of light that makes the diamond a gem of fiery brilliance and beauty.

an ideal husband and his love for Mary was worthy of a story-book—he was tender, bold, dashing, and romantic. Certainly his commitment was deserving of a diamond.

Through the years royalty have always celebrated betrothals with diamond rings. Queen Victoria chose Albert as her prince consort largely because of the sentiments he expressed with his gift of a diamond ring. And Queen Elizabeth II, who has a treasury of jewels at her command, prizes above all else the three-carat diamond ring Prince Philip gave her upon their betrothal.

The diamond came to be the symbol of undying love because its invincible and enduring quality was believed to give it special power to assure eternal love.

During colonial days, diamond hoops were in fashion and were worn as "keeper rings" to guard the wedding band. They were the forerunners of the modern matched engagement and wedding ring sets. The diamond rose cluster evolved later, to be followed by the diamond half loop, which was also popular for wedding rings. Finally, the modern diamond solitaire emerged and has remained popular.

Because marriage is such an important occasion, it is understandable that it should be solemnized with a token of the highest value, a diamond ring. Often, this is the first piece of "real jewelry" a young woman will own. Today's woman chooses her diamond ring on the basis of what looks best on her finger and flatters her the most. She considers the style of the setting as well as the shape of the diamond. A large hand is flattered by a good-sized emerald-cut diamond or a graceful swirl setting featuring a central diamond flanked by baguettes. A small hand is made more attractive by a marquise diamond and a simple, uncluttered setting.

It is interesting to note here that the diamond's "foreverness" has been expressed in a variety of ways. It has been regarded as the "capsule of the sun" or the "eternal gem of light," which holds all the brilliance and fire of the sun. It has also been associated with the sun's unchanging promise to rise again every day.

The diamond has also been called "crystallized lightning." Its heart, it once was said, was actually a spark struck from the sword of Mars, the god of war, a belief that attributed to the diamond the invincibility of the ancient divinity. The diamond's sparkling hues have been likened to the rainbow as well. As the rainbow was an expression of God's eternal covenant with man, so the diamond sealed man's eternal covenant with woman. Actually, to the ancients the diamond was possessed of infinity. Sun, god, lightning, or rainbow, the diamond was at the heart of life and as such would persist.

When we say that a diamond is forever, it is literally true. Every diamond on earth today existed millions of years ago and will still be here for millions more. The diamond, the hardest substance in the world, is practically eternal.

NOTABLE DIAMONDS

Large diamonds have always held a certain fascination. This chapter describes some of the biggest and most beautiful diamonds in the world.

The Cullinan

The Cullinan, the biggest gem diamond ever found, weighed 3,601 carats and measures 2 x 2½ x 4 inches. Late one afternoon in 1905 the superintendent of the Premier Mine in Pretoria, South Africa, was making a routine inspection when he was attracted by something reflecting the setting sun. He extracted the crystal, thinking at first that it was a large chunk of glass. Subsequent tests, however, proved it to be a diamond. It

was named after Sir Thomas Cullinan, who had opened the mine.

Some diamond experts believe that the stone was a piece of a much larger diamond that had somehow been broken off. The Transvaal government bought the rough stone for $750,000 and presented it to King Edward VII to mark his sixty-sixth birthday in 1907. Touched by the gift, the king promised to keep it among the crown jewels. It was then sent to Joseph Asscher in Amsterdam for cutting. The yield was nine major gems, ninety-six small brilliants, and more than nine carats of polished fragments. The largest gem, the Great Star of South Africa, weighs 530.20 carats and is mounted in the imperial scepter, which is on permanent display in the Tower of London.

The Koh-i-Noor

The Koh-i-noor, probably one of the earliest large diamonds found in India, was first reported in 1304 in the possession of the Rajah of Malwa. Later, it fell into the hands of the first Mogul emperor, the Sultan Baber, and was passed down to each of the great Moguls, including Shah Jahan, who built the Taj Mahal.

In 1739 Nadir Shah of Persia invaded India and pillaged the city of Delhi, but he failed to find the huge diamond. One of the harem women he questioned told him that the conquered Mogul emperor had hidden it inside his turban. Taking advantage of an Oriental custom, Nadir Shah invited his captive to a feast and suggested that they exchange turbans in friendship. Nadir Shah withdrew to his tent, unrolled the borrowed turban, and released the great gem. He is said to have exclaimed, "Koh-i-noor!"—meaning "mountain of light"—at the sight of it and thus the stone was named.

The gem went back to Persia with Nadir Shah, but he

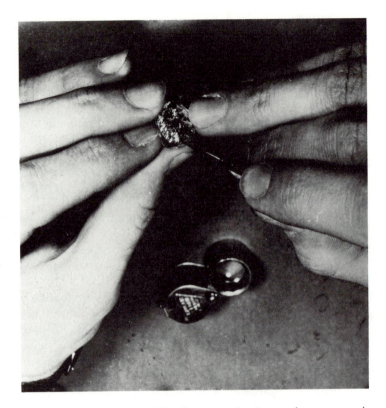

Marking the diamond. The first step in the cutting process is study. The expert examines the diamond through a powerful magnifying glass or "loupe" (shown above) to see how the stone can be cut to keep as much of its original weight as possible. He studies the imperfections within the stone to see how they can be eliminated, for they interfere with the passage of light. Then he marks the diamond with India ink to indicate where the stone must be divided.

was assassinated in 1747. His successors fought bitterly over the diamond. One of them wore it in a bracelet and then had it reset into an armlet, which he wore wherever he went. It was found in the jewel chamber of Lahore, the capital of Punjab, when that state was annexed to British India in 1849, and the East India Company took it as a partial indemnity for the Sikh wars. The following year it was presented to Queen Victoria to mark the 250th anniversary of the company's founding by Queen Elizabeth I.

Valued at $700,000, the Koh-i-noor was displayed at the Crystal Palace Exposition in London in 1851. Since many people were disappointed that the diamond did not show more fire, Victoria decided to have it recut and commissioned a leading diamond-cutter from Amsterdam to come to London to do the job. The cutting reduced the diamond's size from 186 carats to 108.93.

According to the wishes of her Indian subjects, Victoria wore the diamond as a personal ornament, probably giving rise to the superstition that only queens could wear the Koh-i-noor safely. Victoria willed it to her daughter-in-law, Queen Alexandra, who wore it at her coronation in 1902.

In 1911 a new crown was made for the coronation of Queen Mary with the Koh-i-noor as the central stone, and in 1937 the stone was transferred to the crown of Queen Elizabeth (now the Queen Mother) for her coronation. On state occasions, the Queen Mother wears the diamond in the circlet of her crown, but otherwise it remains on display with the other British crown jewels in the Tower of London.

The Regent

One of the finest and most brilliant of all large diamonds, the Regent has had a long and colorful history. The rough stone, weighing 410 carats, was discovered by a slave in an Indian diamond mine in 1701. He escaped to the seacoast, hiding the diamond in the bandages of a self-inflicted leg wound. In return for passage, he offered a ship's captain half the value of the huge stone, but the greedy captain murdered the slave and took the diamond. After selling it to an Indian diamond merchant for about five thousand dollars, the captain squandered the money and in a fit of remorse, hanged himself.

In 1702 the Indian merchant sold the stone for $100,000 to Thomas Pitt, governor of Madras (he was also the grandfather of William Pitt, in whose honor Pittsburgh, Pennsylvania, was named). Pitt sent the diamond to England, where it was cut into a 140.5-carat cushion-shaped gem and became known as the Pitt diamond.

In 1717 it was sold to Philip, duke of Orléans and regent of France, for about $650,000 and was renamed the Regent. It became part of the crown jewels and was worn in the crown of Louis XV at his coronation in 1722.

Removed from the crown, it was worn by Queen Marie Laczinska in her hair. Two generations later, Marie Antoinette often wore the Regent to adorn a large black velvet hat.

During the great robbery of the French crown jewels in 1792 during the early part of the French Revolution, the Regent disappeared and was found many months later in a Paris garret hideaway.

In 1797 the great gem was pledged for money needed to help Napoleon rise to power. He later redeemed it and set it into the hilt of the sword he carried when crowned emperor in 1804. When he went into exile, his second wife, Maria Louise took the Regent away with her. Her father, Emperor Francis I of Austria, however, returned it to France, where it once again became part of the French crown jewels.

Charles X wore the Regent at his coronation in 1825, and the gem remained in the crown until the reign of Napoleon III, who had it placed in a Greek diadem designed for Empress Eugénie.

Many of the French crown jewels were sold at auction in 1887, but the Regent was reserved from the sale and exhibited at the Louvre. Before the Germans invaded Paris in 1940, it was taken to the Château Chambord and hidden behind a stone panel. After World War II the Regent was returned to its place in the Louvre, where it remains on display.

The Hope

The Hope Diamond, 44.5 carats and a rare blue color, is doubtless the most famous diamond in the United States and one of the most celebrated of all. Although the stone has been known in its present form only since 1830, many experts agree that its history probably dates back many centuries.

We have related how the famous French gem expert and traveler, Jean Baptiste Tavernier, is said to have heard about the stone on one of his trips to India and brought it back with him to France in 1642. Just how he obtained it is not clear, but some say he found it mounted in the forehead of a statue of an Indian god. At any rate, when he sold it to Louis XIV in 1668 the diamond was called the Tavernier Blue and weighed more than one hundred carats. The king's jeweler, seeking to improve its brilliance, cut it down to sixty-seven carats, and it became famous as the Blue Diamond of the Crown and the principal gem in the French crown jewels. In 1792, with the Regent, it was stolen from the treasury.

Then, in 1830, a remarkable blue diamond weighing 44.5 carats appeared on the London market and was purchased for the gem collection of Henry Philip Hope. The stone had apparently been cut from the diamond that had disappeared thirty-eight years earlier.

After Hope's death in 1839, the stone become the possession of his nephew, Henry Thomas Hope, who displayed it at the Crystal Palace Exposition in 1851 as the Hope diamond. When his wife died in 1887, she bequeathed it to her youthful grandson, Lord Hope, who married an American actress, May

Yohe, in 1894. She later had a replica of the famous stone made for an unsuccessful stage comeback, and since Hope was heavily in debt he sold the stone to help pay off his obligations.

The diamond changed hands several times. In 1908 Abid Hamid II, sultan of Turkey, bought it for $400,000 but sold it when threatened by a revolution. In 1911, Pierre Cartier acquired it in Paris and sold it to Edward B. McLean for $154,000 to give to his wife. Despite stories about the bad luck it had brought previous owners, Mrs. McLean never considered the stone unlucky.

Following her death in 1947, Harry Winston, a New York gem merchant, bought the stone for $179,920 and presented it to the Smithsonian Institution in Washington, D.C., where it is now on display.

The Orloff

The origin of the Orloff is shrouded in mystery. Some say that it was actually the Great Mogul, which was among the precious gems carried off by the Persians when they captured Delhi in 1739. It has even been suggested that the Orloff, the Great Mogul, and the Darya-i-nur, which was said to have suffered the same fate, may all be the same stone.

Another story has it that the stone was stolen on a stormy night by a French soldier from the eye of an idol in a Brahman temple in southern India. After deserting his squadron and fleeing with the stone, he sold it for $10,000 to an English sea captain who took it to London and sold it to a Persian merchant named Khojeh. In 1775 the diamond turned up in Amsterdam and was bought by Prince Gregory Orloff for $450,000.

In an effort to regain his place as the favorite of Empress Catherine II, Orloff presented her with the 189.6-carat gem. Although Catherine accepted the gift, she refused to reinstate him to his former position of power.

Catherine never wore the Orloff, but instead had it mounted on top of the double eagle in the imperial scepter. To this day it remains in the same setting and is housed in the Soviet Union's diamond treasury in the Kremlin.

The Jubilee

Many gem experts believe that the 245.35-carat Jubilee is the most perfectly cut of all large diamonds. Its facets are so exact that it can be balanced in the culet point, which is less than two millimeters across.

It was found in the Jagersfontein Mine in South Africa in 1895 and weighed 650.8 carats in the rough. At that time it was called the Reitz diamond after the president of the Orange Free State at that time. When it was cut in 1897 to its present size, it emerged a pure-white cushion-shaped brilliant and was renamed the Jubilee because that was the year of Queen Victoria's Diamond Jubilee.

The Jubilee was displayed at the Paris Exposition of 1900 and shortly afterward was sold to Sir Dorab Tata, a leading Indian industrialist. Upon his death it was acquired by Paul-Louis Weiller, a prominent Paris manufacturer, who has displayed it at various exhibits.

The Florentine

The history of the Florentine, too, is veiled in mystery. According to legend, this great yellow diamond was worn by Charles the Bold, duke of Burgundy, in 1477 when he fell at the battle of Nancy. A soldier found the diamond on the duke's body and, thinking it was glass, sold it to a priest for a florin. It has since changed hands many times, and was once owned by Pope Julius II.

In 1657 Tavernier visited the Medici family in Florence, where the duke of Tuscany showed him a clear yellow diamond. The description given by Tavernier of the duke's stone, however, does not tally with what is known about the yellow diamond worn by Charles the Bold, and it may not have been the same gem. From the Medicis, the Florentine passed to the house of Austria through Francis of Lorraine, who became grand duke of Tuscany in 1737, and his wife, Maria Theresa of Austria, who is said to have worn it as a brooch. After the fall of the Austrian Empire, the family took the crown jewels, including the brooch containing the Florentine diamond, into exile with them in South America. In the 1920s the Florentine supposedly entered the United States and was recut and sold, but this is uncertain.

When the Germans invaded Austria during World War II, they carried off from Vienna a diamond that the American authorities returned at the end of the conflict. It is possible, however, that this particular diamond is the one that once adorned the Hapsburg crown, the Austrian Yellow Brilliant. Other names by which the Florentine was known include the Tuscan, the Grand Duke of Tuscany, and the Austrian. The Florentine weighs 137.27 carats.

The Jonker

Just after a heavy rain, a hitherto luckless diamond-digger named Jacobus Jonker picked up a 726-carat stone in the alluvial diggings a few miles from Sir Thomas Cullinan's Premier Mine near Pretoria. It was considered by some experts to have been the finest gem ever found. A few days later Jonker sold it to the Diamond Corporation in South Africa for $315,000.

It was subsequently sold to Harry Winston, the New York gem dealer, for a reported $700,000 and displayed at various museums throughout the country. In time the stone was cut by Lazare Kaplan, the American expert, who produced twelve gems weighing 358 carats in all. The largest of these, which is known as the Jonker, an emerald cut weighing 142.9 carats, was later recut to 125.65 and also exhibited in many cities.

In 1949, when the Jonker was sold to King Farouk of Egypt, it was valued at about $1 million. When Farouk was deposed in 1952, however, the Jonker disappeared, and was later reported to have been sold to Queen Ratna of Nepal. In 1973, it appeared at an auction in Hong Kong, and was bought by a Japanese industrialist.

DIAMOND IMITATIONS

Like the ancient alchemists who dreamed of making gold from base metals, our modern wizards have made many attempts to imitate the gem diamond in the laboratory. The products derived bear a variety of names that can often mislead the unwary into thinking that they are natural diamonds. They are, for example, often called "man-made" or "simulated," but the fact is that they are not diamonds at all.

In 1948 synthetic rutile was accidentally discovered during a search for a better whitener than lead oxide for paint and other products. A single form of titanium oxide, synthetic rutile has a fuzzy brilliance, is dull, and always has a yellowish tinge. With its enormous dispersion and high refractive index, it has been offered under a great many trade names.

In 1953 another titanium compound, strontium titanate, was introduced. This substance, unknown in nature, had the advantage of being more nearly colorless, singly refractive, and of a much more believable dispersion. Like synthetic rutile, however, this newer material suffers from a lack of hardness and does not really take a fine polish. Furthermore, it is so difficult to work that many of these stones are not cut with full diamond faceting. With twice the dispersion of a diamond, strontium titanate shows so much fire that it is easily distinguishable from a diamond.

Various attempts to improve the wearability of these stones have been made. However, both titanium compounds, in addition to being soft, are brittle. This was one of the factors that mitigated against the acceptance of white zircons as diamond imitations.

Synthetic white sapphire and synthetic white spinel have also made their appearances as diamond imitations, but their lack of fire and brilliance give them only superficial resemblance to a diamond. Other materials that lack fire and brilliance but that might confuse the layman nevertheless include colorless beryl, quartz, topaz, glass, and various foilbacks such as rhinestone. The spinel loses brilliance when immersed in water, whereas a diamond does not.

A recently developed substance known as synthetic yttrium aluminum garnet has a relatively low refractive index and does not appear as brilliant, even with the most accurate cutting and polishing possible. This material, known as YAG, though somewhat brittle, is harder than any other imitation except synthetic sapphire. When dipped in mineral oil, this stone becomes transparent; a diamond that has been similarly treated still shows its characteristic brilliance, although somewhat diminished. Like other diamond imitations, YAG usually does not have as fine a polish as a diamond, nor is it faceted with as fine precision.

Another recent diamond imitation known as GGG is synthetic gadolinium gallium garnet. It has rounded facet junctions and sometimes has a tendency to turn brownish.

While any colorless material may be regarded as a possible diamond imitation, there are many important gemological differences between diamond imitations and true diamonds.

Hardness. Even synthetic sapphire, the hardest diamond imitation is infinitely softer than a diamond. Strontium titanate, the material most used for diamond imitations, has a hardness of five on the Mohs' scale, which means it can be scratched by ordinary kitchen cleanser. Thus, the wearability of most diamond imitations is limited.

Cutting, Faceting, and Polishing. Because of their relative softness and because of economic factors, diamond imitations are not cut, faceted, or polished with the fine precision of a diamond.

Fire and Brilliance. While the titanium compounds have a higher dispersion factor than diamond (which makes them instantly recognizable as imitations), they can lose their luster after a period of wear.

Specific Gravity. Because of the difference in specific gravity between the most popular imitations of diamond, the prices per carat of the imitations can be misleading to anyone contemplating an imitation to match a specific diamond size. For instance, if a customer owns a 3.5-carat diamond and wishes a comparable size strontium titanate, he or she will have to purchase one in excess of 5 carats.

Value. Diamond imitations do not have the lasting value of a diamond.

Diamonds for sawing. Each diamond has a grain, like that of wood, apparent to the expert. In most diamonds, the first division is against the grain, and so is made by sawing. The diamond is mounted in a holder called a "dop." In this picture, the four loose stones are all marked for sawing, and the three larger diamonds are in dops, with the markings visible. The dop at the lower right holds one part of a diamond after sawing; the other part is to the left.

Sawing a diamond. The holder with its diamond is clamped into an arm above the saw so that the blade will cut along the marked line. The phosphorbronze saw blade, only 35/10,000ths of an inch thick, has an edge on which a paste of diamond dust and oil creates a cutting surface. The blade turns at high speed, and the diamond is held against it by gravity, sinking as the blade cuts through. Even a small diamond takes hours to be sawed through, and a large diamond may take days.

Sawing many diamonds. Because it takes so long to saw even a small diamond, a diamond cutting factory must have banks of saws going at one time to keep up production. Once the diamond is set on the saw blade, the operation appears to be virtually automatic, but it is not. A skilled sawyer must check each saw at frequent intervals to make sure that the cut is going properly and that the blade is running evenly. Even tiny diamonds, as small as a crystal of sugar, can be divided by sawing.

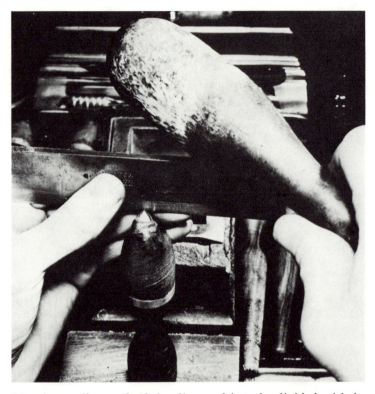

Cleaving a diamond. If the diamond is to be divided with its grain, it is set into a dop and a groove is scratched into it with another diamond. Only a diamond can cut a diamond. The cleaving knife, a special blade of steel, is set into the groove and is tapped lightly with a palm wood hammer. If the stone has been properly marked and grooved, it splits cleanly along the cleavage plane. But if the marking and grooving are only a little bit off, the tap of the mallet can shatter the stone into bits.

Cleaved diamond. When the cutter has properly studied the diamond, it will cleave into two clean pieces like those shown here. Some of the famous diamonds that have been cleaved are: the 3,106-carat Cullinan, the 995.20-carat Excelsior and the 726-carat Jonker.

Girdling the diamond. After the diamond is divided, each part is finished as a separate gem. The next step is "girdling" or "bruting," shaping the diamond at its greatest width. For the round or "brilliant" cut, this is done by mounting the stone on a lathe that revolves at high speed and rounding it with another diamond held in a long stick. Diamonds to be finished in other shapes—marquise, oval, pear-shape, emerald-cut and others—are also girdled but by a different process.

Facets for the diamond. The final step in cutting a diamond is grinding its facets, or planes. Most diamonds have 58 facets, 33 above the girdle and 25 below, each set at a precise angle to its neighbors. For this operation the stone is set in a holder against a revolving iron disk impregnated with oil and diamond dust. Because variations of even a fraction of a degree in the facet angles can reduce the brilliance of a diamond, the cutter will use his skill and years of experience to check this operation continually.

Shapes of finished diamonds. These finished diamonds, in all their beauty, are ready to be set in precious jewelry. From top to bottom, their shapes are the brilliant-cut or round, the emerald-cut, the marquise, the oval, the heart and pear-shape. The kimberlite, on top, is the ore in which diamonds are found. It holds a rough diamond, similar to the ones from which the finished diamonds were fashioned.

Line drawing of Koh-i-noor in its original setting.

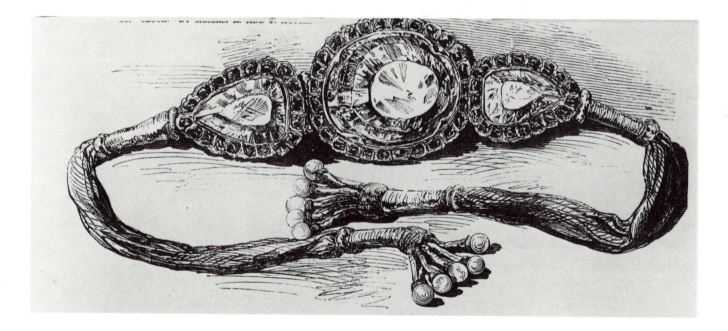

Cullinan Diamond in the rough and the nine principle stones cut from it. The largest, Cullinan I, or Great Star of Africa, weighs 530 carats and is in the British Scepter.

The Hope Diamond

Diamond ring (round cut) and rough diamond in background

"Star of Independence" (75.52 cts.)

"Indore" diamond earclips (46.39 cts. and 44.14 cts.)

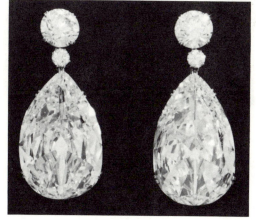

The Jubilee

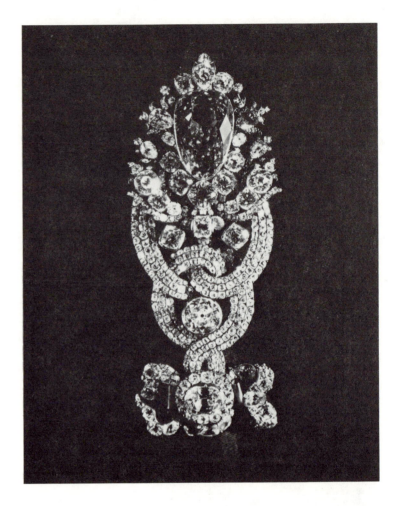

Dresden Green

The Great Chrysanthemum

The Cullinan I or the Great Star of Africa

Diamond and emerald necklace with teardrop designs

The Pearl: Queen of Gems

Man's perpetual delight in the pearl has enriched our literature with countless tales of drama, romance, and beauty that hark back to the dawn of history. The pearl is probably the oldest gem known to us. It is believed that the first of these gems was found off the coast of India about four thousand years ago. It is the most valuable gem that comes from the sea and is produced by an organic process.

Pearls, it was once said, are the tears of the angels. Long before the beauty of polished stones became a reality, pearls were a mark of distinction, of wealth and power. Pearls have always been beloved by royalty, and celebrated families all over the world have passed down pearls from generation to generation.

In religious faiths pearls are regarded as synonymous with divine beauty. The Talmud, the book of Jewish law, describes the coats that God made for Adam and Eve as being "as beautiful as pearls." The Koran relates that those admitted to the celestial kingdom are given tents of pearl, and the New Testament speaks of St. Peter before the fabled pearly gates.

According to a Hindu legend, the god Krishna brought a pearl from the sea for his daughter's wedding day. In Greek mythology Zeus' wife, Hera, was decorated with pearls, and Aphrodite, goddess of love and beauty, possessed a pearl-embroidered girdle that had the power of inspiring love. The Romans virtually worshiped pearls and lavishly bedecked the temple of Venus with them as well as decorating their own jewelry and furniture.

The largest pearl in existence is believed to be the 605-carat fabulous Pearl of Asia, found by Persian divers in 1628. Mogul emperor Shah Jahan bought it for the wife for whom he built the Taj Mahal and the Pearl Mosque. One hundred years later the Pearl of Asia was known to be among the treasures of C'ien Lung, the fourth Manchu emperor of China, who took it with him to his grave in 1799. Grave robbers unearthed it in 1900, and eighteen years later it showed up in Hong Kong as security for a loan by the Catholic Board of Foreign Missions.

The loan was defaulted, and the Pearl of Asia next appeared in Paris after World War II. Its present whereabouts are unknown.

Another ancient pearl is the 200-grain gem from the famous Peacock Throne of Shah Jahan's son, Aurangzeb. The throne was built in the seventeenth century. In Central and South America excavations have unearthed pearls estimated to be a thousand years old but which still retain their beauty.

After the fall of Rome, Constantinople became the great pearl center of the world, and during the Byzantine era the display of pearls increased. Not only were pearls used to adorn people, but they also were set in ecclesiastical robes, statues, books, sacred vessels, and temples.

During the Middle Ages pearls were prized in Europe. They rose steadily in popularity and prestige, and Renaissance families vied with one another to accumulate great quantities of them. The more pearls a family owned and wore, the higher its status.

When a suitor came to ask for the hand of Lucrezia Borgia, her father plunged his hand into a large box of pearls and ran his fingers through them. "All these are for her," he said to the young man as he gave his consent and presented him with the pearls. "I desire that in all Italy she shall be the princess with the most beautiful pearls and the greatest number."

So important were pearls in fashion that men as well as women wore them. In Renaissance and Reformation portraits, the dominant position of pearls is easily discernible. Pearls are visible about the waist as well as on the neck and wrists, and some paintings show pearls on hairnets and on the toes of slippers.

Elizabeth of Bavaria, the wife of Charles VI of France, entered Paris in 1385 wearing a headdress studded with pearls and other jewels. Catherine de Medici possessed one of the largest pearl collections in the world at the time of her marriage to the duke of Orleans who later became Henri II of France. It had been given to her by her uncle, Pope Clement VII, as part of her dowry.

Sixteenth-century queens and courtesans were virtually clothed in pearls, and Mary, Queen of Scots, was said to have had one of the finest sets of pearls in all of Europe. Paintings of her cousin, Elizabeth I, show the queen in dresses so heavily weighted with pearls that she must have found it difficult to move.

As a matter of fact, pearls were so popular between the thirteenth and sixteenth centuries that special laws were enacted to limit their use. In some countries only those of the highest-ranking nobility were allowed to wear them, but the gem was so greatly loved that people found ways to evade the laws.

Like most gems, pearls were credited with magical powers. They were generally used as amulets symbolic of health and longevity. This belief led in time to their use by medieval doctors as medicines for their wealthy patients. Of the benefits of pulverized and dissolved pearls, a thirteenth-century Spanish physician wrote: "The pearl is most excellent in the medical art for it is of great help in palpitation of the heart and those who are sad or timid or in every sickness caused by melancholia because it purifies the blood, clears it, and removes all impurities."

Advances in medical science during the succeeding centuries and the decreasing reliance on magic have led to less emphasis on the popularity of the gem as a cure-all. At the same time the expansion of the art of cutting and polishing precious stones weakened the domination of the pearl. Nevertheless, queens, noblewomen, and courtesans continued to wear pearls in profusion. Queen Alexandra wore them liberally at the coronation of her husband, King Edward VII, and portraits of contemporary ladies of high rank show them bedecked with many pearls, usually in the form of multiple-strand necklaces.

THE PEARL INDUSTRY

Fresh-water pearls have been found in many American rivers, and there is evidence that many of the tribes that lived here used them for adornment, too. Columbus' landing at San Salvador in 1492 was marked by the discovery of quantities of pearls, which in time became one of the many attractions of the New World. During the two centuries following the discovery of America, the Spanish merchants who had access to these pearls supplied the world with them and became fabulously wealthy.

Pearls often are found in mollusks living in fresh-water streams. Diving for pearls has long been a lucrative occupation in Ireland, and Scottish rivers were the source of the lovely pearl set owned by Mary, Queen of Scots. In 1857 a magnificent pink pearl weighing ninety-three grains was found near the city of Paterson, New Jersey, in a brook. It was sent to Paris, where it was eventually bought by Empress Eugenie. Fresh-water pearls have also been found in other parts of the United States.

Pearls from these sources, however, are not usually of top quality or size. The waters of India, Sri Lanka, Australia, and Tahiti contain pearls, but the most valuable ones come from the Persian Gulf.

The Persian Gulf for more than three thousand years has been a source of the finest natural (or Oriental) pearls with a delicate pinkish hue that makes them outstanding in beauty. Many white pearls come from the waters of Australia or Panama. Creamy beige pearls often are found in Venezuelan waters; and the rare black pearl, sometimes with a green cast, come from Tahiti, Panama and the Gulf of California.

Salt-water pearls are found in many other shades as well. The extremely rare iridescent is exceptionally beautiful, tinted with shades of color ranging from pink to violet.

It takes from one to three years for an oyster to produce a gem pearl. Its base is either an irritant that has been washed into the shell or a parasite or other microscopic organism that the oyster cannot expel. The oyster automatically coats the foreign body with a smooth film called nacre to reduce irritation. The accretion of nacre is part of the process by which the pearl enlarges, layer upon layer. The most lustrous pearls are those that have the thinnest layers of nacre, one upon the other.

The color of pearls is affected by many factors, among them the mineral content of the waters and the food supply of the oyster. However, the pearl always has a color identical to the lining of the shell. A black pearl, for example, comes from a black-lined shell. The pearl's iridescent quality is an optical phenomenon caused by the interference of light rays reflected from the delicately layered surface of the pearl.

Pearls found inside the body of the oyster are considered the finest, as those adhering to the shell have a flattened side. Pearls of the greatest value are absolutely round and have a flawless surface. The most desirable are pinkish in color with a faint undertone of cream.

Primitive methods for gathering pearls are still used in the Persian Gulf. Divers continue to bring up pearl-bearing oysters in the manner of their forebears. They still dive with a rope and basket and refuse to use the modern diving equipment or motorized boats now available to them. The process is slow. The divers descend to the ocean floor and collect the oysters in baskets. After remaining underwater as long as their lungs permit, they return to the surface. The oysters are opened later and whatever pearls have been found are sorted by grade and size. Rarely are more than a few valuable round pearls by a diver found during an entire season of diving. Natural or Oriental pearls command the highest prices because of their great scarcity and the arduous labor required to gather them.

CULTURED PEARLS

The idea of duplicating the production of pearls has long been one of man's obsessions. As long ago as the thirteenth century, the Chinese were producing cultured pearls of a sort by inserting tiny images of Buddha under the shells of pearl mollusks, which in time covered them with layers of nacre. But it was not until the beginning of the twentieth century that the birth of the modern cultured pearl industry in Japan led to mass production of such pearls.

After considerable experimentation, the Japanese found that a certain variety of oyster in their waters, the *Pinctada martensi*, could be caused to produce cultured pearls with some help from man. Each oyster is opened and a small mother-of-pearl bead is inserted with a sliver of living tissue from another oyster. The oyster is then returned to the water in a little basket and kept suspended in it for eighteen months to three years. The pearl farmer keeps a careful watch on the oysters and protects them from natural enemies and hazards. In the winter he moves them to warmer waters so that they can mature in a constant and nearly ideal temperature.

At the end of the waiting period the oysters are brought up. When the shells are opened, the pearl farmer may find a lustrous, perfectly rounded pearl or, of course, he may find an irregularly shaped pearl or none at all. The pearls of value are cleaned, graded, and sorted by size and grade.

In the Lake Biwa region of Japan, fresh-water cultured pearls are produced in clams without using any bead. The pearls are generally long and oval in shape and are ideally suited for certain natural-looking jewelry designs.

SIMULATED PEARLS

Simulated or imitation pearls are manufactured by coating beads of glass, plastic, or other material with a substance that gives them a pearly glow. The fish-scale essence that is often used is comparable in appearance to the nacre of the genuine or cultured pearl. The quality, color, and luster of simulated pearls vary considerably and depend on the number of layers of coating and the base used. The better pearls are thoroughly dried between each dipping in a room where the humidity and temperature are controlled to insure perfect drying conditions. The finer grades are polished between each dipping with a chamois and fine polishing powder.

Other methods of manufacturing pearls utilize hollow glass or plastic beads coated on the inside with fish-scale essence or with a synthetic fish-scale luster.

JEWELERS' STANDARDS FOR PEARLS

Jewelers judge pearls on the following standards:

Luster. Luster depends on the reflection of light from the surface of the pearl. Generally, the more coatings, the deeper and more brilliant the luster.

Orient. Orient is the result of the refraction of light from the translucency of the pearl surface through the various layers of nacre. It enhances the luster of the pearl.

A Japanese pearl farm
41

Catching oysters

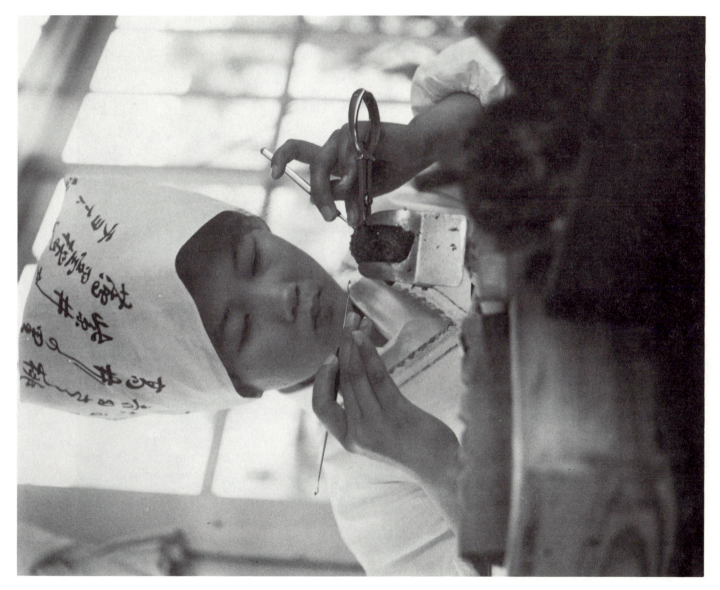

Removing pearl from oyster

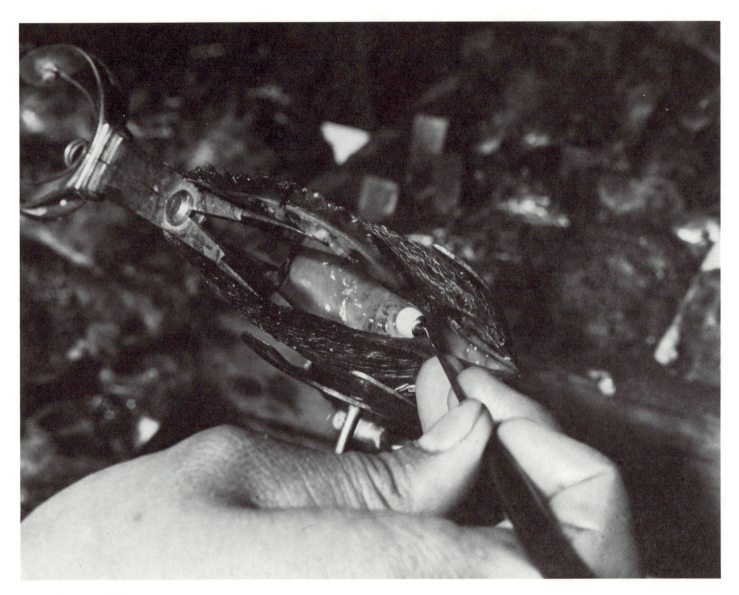

Removing pearl from oyster

Choosing pearls for stringing
45

Single pearl

Stringing pearls

47

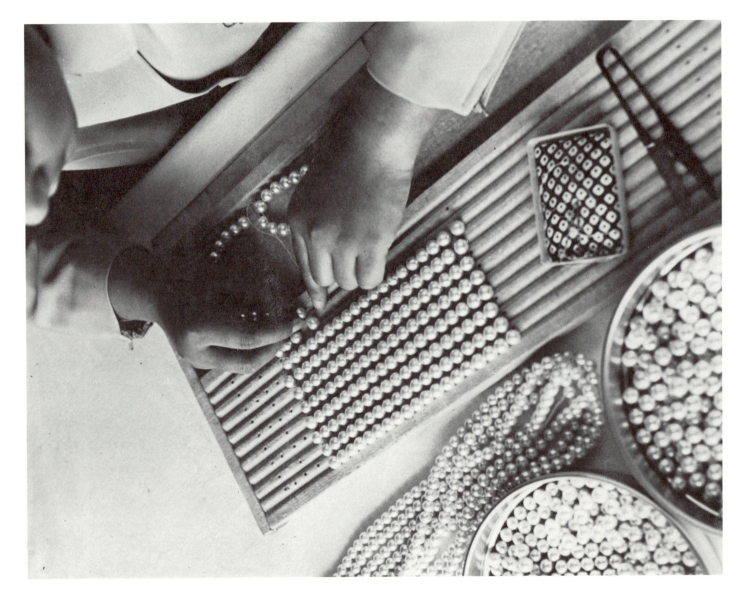

Woman stringing pearls

Cleanliness. Cleanliness refers to the absence of blemishes; the fewer blemishes, the higher the value of the pearl.

Color. Pearls come in an almost infinite variety of hues and shades, ranging from pink to gold through green, blue, silver, and black. The best color for any woman is the one that flatters her the most. Rosé tones complement a fair complexion, darker shades complement creamy or olive skins.

Size. The size of a pearl is measured by its diameter in millimeters, a millimeter being approximately one-twenty-fifth of an inch. Generally, prices of pearls increase with size, because large pearls are scarcer than small ones. Formerly the unit of weight was the grain, equal to 50 milligrams or one-fourth of a carat. Fine pearls are sometimes measured in this way. In the cultured pearl industry, the standard of weight is the momme, a Japanese term pronounced "mommie," each weighing three-fourths of an ounce. A 6-millimeter pearl necklace, for example, would weigh about 5 momme.

Shape. Pearls are found in many shapes. The round pearl is perfectly spherical, while the baroque is irregular in form. Other types include pear, drop, button, and mobé (a half-round).

Matching. No two pearls are exactly alike. Most necklaces are the result of a careful blending of pearls that appear to match in color, luster, and size. The matching of pearls is a fine art.

STYLES IN PEARL NECKLACES

Many terms are used to refer to various styles of necklaces.

Graduated. A graduated necklace is one in which pearls of gradually increasing size are strung, with the smaller pearls near the clasp and the largest at the center.

Uniform. A uniform necklace is composed of pearls of nearly equal size.

Choker. A choker is a uniform pearl necklace that rests just above the wearer's collarbone.

Princess. A princess-length necklace measures eighteen inches.

Matinee. As its name implies, the matinee is a dressier style, twenty to twenty-four inches in length.

Opera. Opera length pearls are even more formal, as long as twenty-eight to thirty inches.

Bib. A bib is a necklace of more than three strands.

Rope. A rope is a necklace forty-five or more inches in length. A lariat is an open-ended long strand with a detachable clasp.

Because pearls are appropriate for every occasion from morning until night and every season of the year, they are worn everywhere by fashionable women. Pearls are always flattering and can be brought up to date by redesigning. Pearl jewelry today includes rings, pins, pendants, bracelets, and earrings as well as necklaces. And many men wear pearl cuff links, studs, and tie tacks.

CARE OF PEARLS

To keep pearls beautiful, it is necessary to follow just a few simple rules:

—Pearls should be strung with silk threads and with knots between the gems. These knots keep them from touching and damaging each other. The string on which pearls are strung should not be allowed to get wet, and they should be restrung at least once a year, preferably twice.

—Never put on your pearls until after you have applied

Freshly strung pearls, various sizes

Pearl necklace, ring, and pins

makeup and perfume, as the chemicals in these can harm the gems. For the same reason, never immerse pearls in a chemical or acid solution.

—Protect pearls from perspiration, dust, and dampness by wiping them with a chamois after each wearing and keeping them in a closed, soft-lined box when not in use.

—Handle your pearls gently. Avoid dropping them or allowing them to strike any hard surface.

—Wear your pearls often. Body contact is said to make them glow more and more beautifully. There is an old super-stition that pearls lose their luster when their owner dies, that they need love and care to attain and maintain their greatest potential for beauty.

The pearl is the birthstone of the month of June and still, as in days of old, signifies health and longevity:

"Who comes with summer to this earth
And owes to June her day of birth
With ring of pearl upon her hand
Can health, long life, and wealth command."

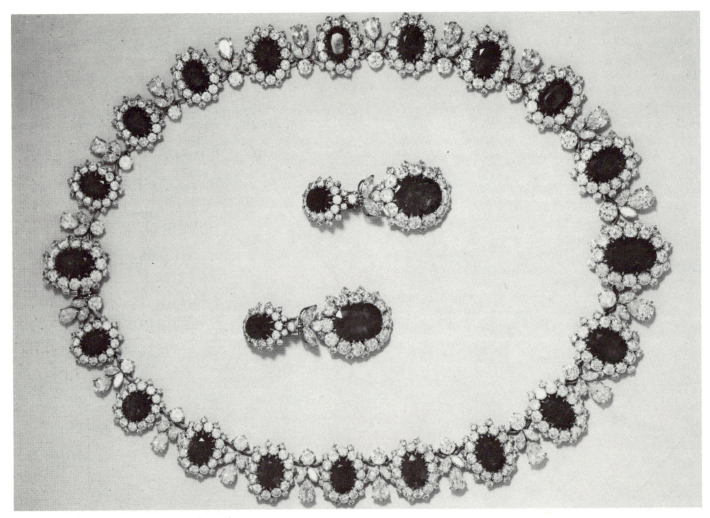

Ruby and diamond necklace and earrings

the Ruby, the Sapphire, & the Emerald

The ruby, the sapphire, and the emerald display vivid shades of red, blue, and green. Their dramatic colors give the three stones their rare and special beauty.

THE RUBY

According to legend, the ruby contains the original spark of life; and the nineteenth-century writer John Ruskin described it as "the loveliest stone of which I have knowledge." Both the ruby and the sapphire are transparent varieties of corundum, the mineral that is next to but below the diamond in hardness. The red variety is called ruby, and all transparent corundum that is not red is known as sapphire. Sapphire is usually blue but is also found in many other hues, including pink, gold, green, white, and black. Minor amounts of chromium oxide or titanium oxide color the corundum red or blue and determine whether it is ruby or sapphire.

The ruby is one of the rarest and most valuable gems in the world. In speaking of the gifts of God, Job said, "The price of wisdom is above rubies." Many superlatives have been ap-plied to the ruby by historians and writers. The ancients called it the "lord of gems" and the "stone of life" and attributed to it many special powers. The Hindus called it the "king of precious stones" and valued it more than they did any other gem. They divided rubies into four castes according to grade in the belief that a gem of the highest caste would shield its owner from bad luck and permit him to live fearlessly among his enemies.

During the days of the early Romans many red stones were mistakenly called rubies because of a lack of gemological knowledge. Pliny warned that red stones could easily be counterfeited by the art and skill of lapidaries who put a foil beneath them "to make them brilliant and glitter like fire."

For centuries the Hindus believed that white (colorless) sapphire was an "unripe" ruby that would eventually mature. Burmese gem miners held that pale-colored rubies buried in the earth would gradually change to a fine red. Ceylonese miners considered flawed stones to be "overripe." The Burmese had an old legend about the unreachable "blazing red" stones in a bottomless valley that could not be ventured. Natives threw pieces of meat into the valley to lure vultures, in the hope that some stones would cling to the meat and then be recovered by killing the vultures that had feasted on the meat.

The ruby was thought to make its owner invulnerable. To release its power, however, the stone had to be inserted in the owner's flesh through an intentional wound. It was said that a warrior who voluntarily suffered such pain would then be immune to the sword, spear, and gun. Another familiar superstition associated with the gem was that anyone who carried the stone as a talisman into fierce battle would emerge unscathed.

The ruby was also said to cure many illnesses, including skin ailments, hemorrhages, and inflammations. A necklace of rubies strung on silk and worn against the skin was supposed to ward off deadly venom and make the skin impenetrable to the sharpest blade.

The Bible tells of the ruby placed on Aaron's neck in these words: "The ruby, called the lord of gems; the highly prized, the dearly beloved ruby, so fair with its gay color." According to the Arabic dreambooks, to dream of rubies is to be destined for great happiness; the future holds good news, good fortune, and good health for such a dreamer.

Among the ancient Chinese, a mandarin's rank was indicated by the color of the gem he wore. A red stone, preferably a ruby; was a mark of the highest status. Marco Polo told of a monarch who owned a red gem "four inches long and thick as a finger" for which the emperor of China offered an entire city in payment, but the monarch stubbornly refused. "If all the treasures of the world were laid at my feet, I would not part with this jewel!" he replied.

Within the ruby the ancients saw fire, everlasting and inextinguishable. This eternal flame, they were convinced, could never be hidden, not even beneath many layers of clothing. Potential thieves, therefore, avoided rubies, giving rise to still another belief: The gem would protect its owner from theft.

Some even thought the fire of the ruby was so powerful that a gem dropped into water would cause the water to boil.

In the fourteenth century the unknown compiler of a book of travels who called himself Sir John Mandeville wrote of the ruby: "The fortunate owner of a brilliant ruby will live in peace and concord with all men; neither his land nor his rank can be taken from him." But for the ruby to do its good work he said, its owner had to have it set in a ring, bracelet, or brooch and wear it only on his left side.

The ruby gets its name from the Latin word for "red," but rubies are found in a wide spectrum of colors that range from pale pink to deep purple tones. Only transparent corundum of medium to dark red and purple-red is properly called ruby. Very light tones of red are correctly called pink sapphire. The coloring is not always uniform. Stones of darker color are often termed male and those of light shades, female.

Rubies are found chiefly in Burma, Thailand, and Sri Lanka. The finest stones come from Burma. These stones, mined in the Moguk area about ninety miles from Mandalay, are generally bright, clear red, which is the most prized color and is known as "pigeon blood." Originally, these fine rubies were found in the lodes of granular limestone on the sides of the hills, but through the years the limestone outcrops have been eroded, and rubies are now found in clay and gravel washed into the riverbed.

Large rubies are extremely rare and cost much more than diamonds of comparable size and quality. Clear stones are worth more than some translucent ones with silky interiors (due to a fibrous content). The surface of the latter, when cut into a domed, unfaceted style called *cabochon*, reflects streaks of light. These are the star rubies, which contain long, narrow crystals arranged in three sets of parallel threads that intersect at angles of sixty degrees. Star rubies, after being cut, appear to have a star of radiant white light inside. The "silk" in these stones makes them slightly less transparent and tends to gray the color and lighten it.

While large flawless or nearly flawless rubies are extremely rare and command exceedingly high prices, many small but beautiful rubies are available at comparatively moderate cost. When combined with diamonds, emeralds, sapphires, or other stones, they greatly enhance jewelry designs.

The hardness of the ruby makes it durable and enables it to take a very high polish. Its brilliant color is brought out by cutting. The quality of the cutting of a ruby is an important factor in its value, since it affects the apparent "spread" of the stone as well as its color and brilliance. The "spread" is the width of the stone at the girdle, or outer edge, and this can affect the gem's beauty. A stone of fine quality may be cut with a deep pavilion and, when compared with one of equal weight and beauty but of shallower cut, may be less valuable. On the other hand, a stone cut so shallowly that the center area seems lusterless and without brilliance is not as valuable as one with more exacting cutting proportions. In essence, the value of a ruby depends upon color, freedom from flaws, fine polish, and the proportions of its cut.

Magnificent rubies are on view at various museums throughout the world. The *Edwardes* ruby, a 167-carat crystal, is on display at the British Museum of Natural History; and one of the largest star rubies in existence, the 100-carat Edith Haggin de Long star ruby, may be seen at the American Museum of Natural History. The 138-carat, fine-quality Rosser Reeves star ruby is at the Smithsonian Institution.

Many lovely natural rubies were owned by royalty. The Empress Josephine received from Napoleon a parure (matching set) of rubies to soothe the pain of divorce. Carlota, wife of Maximilian, emperor of Mexico, left behind in the palace of Chapultepec her magnificent rubies, which later fell into the hands of the Maderos and were lost in a shipwreck. Elizabeth,

wife of the Emperor Franz Joseph of Austria, always wore a ruby as a talisman but, according to legend, failed to wear it on the morning she was assassinated.

The ruby is the birthstone of July, as this ancient verse of unknown origin proclaims:

> *"The gleaming ruby should adorn*
> *All those who in July are born.*
> *For this they'll be exempt and free*
> *From love's doubts and anxiety."*

The ruby is also Tuesday's stone, the sign of nobility and power of command in a man, and of proper pride in a woman.

THE SAPPHIRE

Formed of the same material as the ruby, the sapphire differs from it only in color. The mythological influence of the sapphire, the gem of wisdom, is deemed to be totally beneficent. The blue of the heavens that it displays made it seem celestial in nature to the ancients. For the Egyptians, the wearing of a sapphire—especially a star sapphire—caused the stars to spin into favorable conjunction.

The sapphire has long been considered the gem most suited to ecclesiastical usage, and its widespread association with religion is most manifest in the Judeo-Christian tradition. As mentioned earlier, Moses was believed to have received the Ten Commandments engraved on a sapphire tablet. King Solomon's seal was a star sapphire, and the blue gem is one of the foundation stones of the Christian New Jerusalem and is held sacred to St. Paul.

The Persians believed that the earth itself rested on an enormous sapphire and that the sky was but a mirror reflecting this foundation. Sapphire was also the gem dedicated to Freya, the Nordic goddess of love, beauty, and fecundity.

The beneficence of the sapphire is said to be always faithful and to protect its first wearer even after the stone itself has gone to a second owner. It was, therefore, regarded as a safeguard against harm and envy from others. Many a king wore the gem around his neck, as did others who could afford one. They regarded the stone as their most powerful defense; it was expected not only to protect life and limb but to banish fraud as well. Such power was it reputed to have that it was said to vanquish venom and exterminate poisonous insects. "And if you put a spider in a box and hold a sapphire of India," said John de Trevisa, the Cornish scholar of the fourteenth century, "the spider is overcome and dieth, as it were suddenly. And this I have often assayed in many and diverse places."

The sapphire was also believed to be a talisman against evil spirits and a healer of boils and diseases of the eyes.

Sapphires come mainly from Burma, Thailand, Kashmir, Sri Lanka, Australia, and the state of Montana. The blue of sapphires can vary greatly, the most prized being the "cornflower" blue tone. The blue color should be deep enough to look rich by day and yet remain a fine glowing blue under artificial light. This is true of many Kashmir stones. Sri Lanka stones are usually pale, while those from Australia are generally so dark that they verge on black. Montana stones are often steely and metallic in appearance. Like diamonds, sapphires come in almost all colors, including yellow, orange, green, violet, pink, and white.

The sapphires that show the curious phenomenon of asterism are known as star sapphires. As in star rubies, effect is caused by a fibrous content called silk in the crystalline structure of the stone. Asterism can occur in almost any color sapphire, though yellow and green are very rare. When the star sapphire is cut in a cabochon (dome) shape, with its surface arching over the structural layers of silk, the interior of the

stone reflects light in the form of a star made up of three intersecting crossbars. Legend has given meaning to the six rays in a star sapphire or ruby and has named them Faith, Hope, Charity, Health, Wealth, and Happiness. Apparently, the fortunate owner of one of these gems is six times blessed.

The value of a star stone depends on its transparency and the definition of its star. Cloudiness or grayishness decreases value. The intersecting rays should be in the center of the stone and the star complete and devoid of any weak or missing rays; it should be well defined and appear to "roll" easily across the surface. It must also have "depth" that appears to come from within the stone.

Fraudulent methods are sometimes used to improve the appearance of star stones. Rubbing the roughened back with an ordinary lead pencil, for example, will darken a star stone and make the star more pronounced. Oil, wax, colorless nail polish, or silica compounds are occasionally used to conceal cracks, fissures, or other imperfections. Since these techniques have only temporary effects, they are definite misrepresentations.

Numerous materials are applied to the base of star stones in an effort to improve their color. These include enamel, various kinds of dyes, lens coatings, and even impure corundum. A few pieces are assembled by cementing synthetic star-sapphire corundum tops to irregular pieces of poor-quality natural sapphire; these are then set in mountings that conceal the separation plane.

To judge the quality of star sapphires as well as rubies, examine the color, star, and proportions. If related flaws are not readily visible to the naked eye, the stone may be regarded as a fine-quality specimen. A star stone that exhibits no defects under ten-power magnification is the exception. Such stones do exist, of course, but they are exceedingly rare and command exceptionally high prices.

Perhaps the most famous and ancient star sapphire is the

"Star of India," which is on display at the American Museum of Natural History in New York. This magnificent specimen weighs 543 carats and is one of the most celebrated stones in all the world. A furor arose when this rare gem was stolen, but it was recovered and returned to the museum.

Sapphire is the birthstone for September and its day is Friday. It signifies magnanimous thoughts and wisdom in a man, deep powers of observation in a woman. Soothsayers predict that Friday will be an auspicious day for love for those who wear a sapphire.

THE EMERALD

The verdant beauty of the emerald was described by the ancients as the captured glow of the firefly. Long dedicated to the goddess Venus, the emerald was believed to have the power to reveal the beloved's fidelity or unfaithfulness:

> *"It is a gem that hath the power to show*
> *If plighted lovers keep their troth or no.*
> *If faithful, it is like the leaves of spring;*
> *If unfaithful, like those leaves withering."*

No other gem in the world possesses the glorious color of the emerald. Unlike some precious stones, the value of a richly colored crystal is immediately obvious. Pliny the Elder said, "No stone has a color that is more delightful to the eye, for whereas the sight fixes with avidity upon the green grass and the foliage of the trees, we have all the more pleasure in looking upon the emerald, there being no green in existence more intense than this. And, of all the precious stones, this is the only one that feeds the sight without satiating it. Neither sunshine, shade, nor artificial light effects any change in its appearance; it has always a softened and graduated brilliancy."

The emerald was conceived to be a magical crystal that could foreshadow the future, sharpen its owner's wits, and expand intelligence; moreover, it brought out the quality of honesty in people and stimulated memory. Those who believed themselves plagued by witchcraft depended on the emerald to thwart the spell of even the most powerful witch. And the emerald was the most oft-used defense against poisons, from those of deadly insects or reptiles to those used in attempts at murder.

Emeralds were also believed to be a panacea for the ills of the eye. The emperor Nero was said to refresh and restore his vision by viewing the violence of the gladiator shows through the cool clarity of a fine emerald. During the Renaissance, goldsmiths and watchmakers suffering from eyestrain after long hours of fine and delicate work would restore their vision by taking time out to gaze at an emerald. Perhaps this is why today so many people wear green-tinted sunglasses.

One ancient theory held that the emerald would make the wearer more economical and therefore more likely to become wealthy. And, according to Roman legend, a marble statue of a lion on the island of Cyprus near the tomb of Hermias had two fine emeralds set into its head. Their gaze fixed on the sea, these emerald "eyes" glittered so brightly and pierced so deeply into the water that all the tuna off the coast were frightened and fled away, out of reach of the nets of the fishermen. For a while, the fishermen could not surmise what had caused their loss, but finally they grew to suspect the emeralds and removed them. Immediately, their catches returned to normal.

When the Spaniards conquered the Incas in Peru, they found an enormous number of beautiful emeralds and demanded to be told their source. But neither persecution nor torture could make the Incas reveal from whence the stones had come. The Spanish set out for themselves to find the source of the stones, but the Incas had carefully eliminated every trace of the mine openings, and jungle growth had rapidly concealed the paths that led to them. It was not until years later that one of the mines was accidentally found in Muzo in Colombia—the source of the finest emeralds in the world to this day.

An interesting anecdote about the early development of these mines tells of a titled Spaniard who received as a reward for services an exclusive mining concession for one of these famous deposits. He expended practically his entire fortune without results. Finally, as a last resort, he followed the suggestion of one of his laborers. To his amazement he found emeralds far exceeding the value of his investment. He selected a large parcel of stones, sailed to England, and invited prospective buyers to examine the emeralds, which he displayed on a large table. The gem dealers were astonished at the quantity and quality of the emeralds and cautiously asked whether any more were to be found at his mines. The Spaniard bragged that the stones were the result of just a few days' labor and that many more remained unmined. The dealers, fearing that a large number of stones would be thrown onto the market, refused to bid even though the seller tried in vain to change his story. His emeralds remained unsold for more than two years, until the dealers had satisfied themselves that the gems offered were likely to be the only products from that particular locality.

Emeralds have rarely been given individual names, even though many have had fascinating historical backgrounds. One of the most famous emeralds is the Devonshire emerald, a 1,383.95-carat uncut Colombian crystal of fine green color. It was given to the sixth duke of Devonshire when he came to Europe after his abdication in 1831 and is on permanent loan to the British Museum of Natural History. A 1,200-carat crystal of fine color known as the Patricia emerald is on display at the American Museum of Natural History in New York.

Probably the most famous single piece of emerald jewelry is the Crown of the Andes, which includes the Atahualpa emerald, a 45-carat stone named after the last Incan king of Peru. The crown, created in 1593 from a solid block of pure gold, was made for the statue of the Madonna in the Cathedral of Popayan. The piece has a long history. In 1650 it was captured by the English, who held it for only three days. In 1812 it became a prize of war during the revolution in which Simon Bolivar freed the South American colonies from Spanish domination. The Crown of the Andes contains 452 stones weighing a total of 1,521 carats and has been exhibited all over the world.

The emerald has had many religious meanings and uses, too. It was the third stone in the breastplate of Aaron, High Priest of Judea, and the fourth foundation stone of the New Testament. Andreas, bishop of Caesarea, wrote: "Its transparency and beauty may not change; we conceive the stone to signify John the Evangel." The substance of the first Moslem heaven is emerald.

Medium-light to medium-dark tones of green beryl are called emerald. Stones that are very light or very light green are properly called green beryl rather than emerald. Emeralds are one of the few gems that are not found in quantity in alluvial deposits.

Despite the fact that emeralds of gem quality are exceedingly rare, crystals have been found in a number of localities throughout the world. The ancient Egyptian mines, the same mines once owned by Cleopatra and mined by primitive methods, have been worked extensively and extend to a depth of more than eight hundred feet. By today's standards, however, the stones it yields are not of high quality.

While the finest emeralds come from Colombia, the gems are also found in Siberia, Brazil, and Rhodesia. The emeralds produced by mines in the Ural Mountains in Siberia are characteristically more yellowish green, more flawed, and slightly lighter in color than Colombian stones. Most of the stones produced in Brazil are more properly classified as green beryl, but some are sufficiently deep in tone to be called emerald.

The most recent discovery of importance occurred in southern Rhodesia in the Sandawana Valley in 1954, when two prospectors seeking beryl discovered some emeralds in an area infested by crocodiles and other wildlife. Most of the stones are small but of a color so intense that they are ideally suited for guard rings and other jewelry.

The step cut is so commonly used for the emerald that this style is usually referred to as the emerald cut. This is especially true if the stone is rectangular in shape, with eight sides and three tiers of facets on top and three tiers on bottom. A square stone of this shape is called a square emerald cut. Heavily flawed stones are usually cut cabochon style or carved. Small stones are often cut into baguettes. The round brilliant cut is rarely used, since it does not show the color of an emerald to best advantage.

To merit top-quality designation, an emerald must be an intense, medium-dark tone of slightly yellowish- or bluish-green and have a soft, velvety appearance with a minimum of flaws. Stones of this quality are exceedingly rare, and much less than 1 percent of them can be classified in this grade. In sizes of two and three carats and larger, they are far more costly than diamonds of the same weight and quality.

Since emeralds have no fire and less brilliance than most gems, beauty and distribution of color are the prime factors in determining their value. Stones in which lighter and darker portions are arranged irregularly or in layers are not as desirable as those that are evenly colored. Usually and ironically, the better the color the less perfect the stone is likely to be. Light to medium-light tones are far less valuable, even when nearly flawless or only slightly flawed. The fine vivid green color and velvety appearance of the emerald occur in no other transparent stone and contribute greatly to its value.

We have mentioned that emeralds have long been associated with love and romance. In the Orient they were first used to decorate the statues of the reigning god or goddess of love and later became symbolic of passionate love. The emerald worn by a man bespeaks great joyousness and that worn by a woman imparts a love of variety. Its day of the week is Wednesday.

Cleopatra's famous emerald mines in Egypt yielded enough emeralds for her to engrave them with her portrait and give them to her many favorites as mementos. Hernando Cortes brought back to Queen Isabella magnificent Peruvian emeralds carved in Mexico. Emeralds were chosen by Napoleon for Empress Josephine as proof of his great love for her. Catherine the Great of Russia, Empress Eugenie, and Queen Victoria were among the many women of royalty who loved and collected emeralds. On the other hand, Julius Caesar was an ardent collector of emeralds because he believed in them as a charm against epilepsy and a cure against eye disease.

Ruby and diamond ring and rough ruby stone

Emerald and diamond ring and rough emerald in background

Sapphire and diamond ring and rough sapphire in background

Birthstones

The previous chapters have shown that men have worn gems not only for personal adornment but also because they believed that gems had magical powers that could protect them against evil and bring good luck. As civilization progressed, however, astrologers began to study gems and to associate them with the planets. Horoscopes were cast at a child's birth to determine his future according to the planet under which he was born, and the signs of the zodiac came to be regarded as a most important influence.

During the Middle Ages and the Renaissance, astrology was looked upon as an established science. Now it was astrologers who recommended certain stones to people and warned them against others. Pearls were deemed unlucky for Elizabeth of England and Mary, Queen of Scots, while Henry VIII's astrologer advised the king to wear the ruby. Many men and women today believe in horoscopes and in wearing an appropriate talisman or lucky stone; others do not believe in astrology but wear a particular stone "just for good luck."

In an earlier chapter, we indicated that the association of a special gem with each month of the year is said to have originated with the twelve precious stones in the breastplate of Aaron. These twelve gems represented the twelve tribes of Israel and were also the foundation stones for each of the twelve apostles in the temple at New Jerusalem.

Later the twelve gems were linked with the twelve signs of the zodiac and eventually came to be associated with the months of the year. In the first century A.D. the historian Flavius Josephus traced the connection between the breastplate, the twelve months of the year, and the zodiac signs and wrote: "And for the twelve stones, whether we understand by them the months or the twelve signs of what the Greeks call the zodiac, we shall not be mistaken in their meaning."

In early times all twelve stones were worn in rotation by the same person to insure maximum protection during each month of the year. Catherine de Medici wore a girdle set with twelve such stones to derive the utmost benefit. The actual wearing of the birthstone appropriate for one's month of birth, however, is believed to have originated in the eighteenth century in Poland when gem traders settled there.

Birthstones were first valued for their special mystical

powers as talismans of good luck, but as lapidary arts and skills developed to enhance their natural beauty, they were worn as attractive gems and jewels as well.

Over the years the lists of birthstones have varied slightly, but the following is the official one adopted by the jewelers in the United States:

Month	Stone	Significance
January	Garnet	Constancy
February	Amethyst	Sincerity
March	Aquamarine or Bloodstone	Courage
April	Diamond	Innocence
May	Emerald	Love
June	Pearl, Alexandrite, or Moonstone	Health
July	Ruby or Star Ruby	Contentment
August	Peridot or Sardonyx	Married Happiness
September	Sapphire and Star Sapphire	Clear Thinking
October	Opal or Tourmaline	Hope
November	Topaz	Fidelity
December	Turquoise or Zircon	Prosperity

JANUARY: THE GARNET

Garnets come in practically every color except blue; they range from pale orange to dark red and violet. The garnet at its best is a deep, rich red or purple-red.

Early scientists named the stone from the Latin *granatus*, which means "seedlike," because garnet crystals in a rock reminded them of the shape and color of pomegranate seeds. The garnet was known thousands of years before the Christian era and in ancient writings is probably mentioned as ruby or carbuncle. The latter term is still applied to the red garnet cut in the cabochon form.

Not only was the garnet regarded as the gem of faith, constancy, and truth, but it was believed also to possess many curative powers. At one time it was ground into a powder and used as a poultice, for red garnet was said to relieve fever, and yellow garnet was the prescription for jaundice.

Asians used garnets as bullets in the belief that their strong red color would inflict a deadly wound. Such bullets were used in India in 1892 during the rebellion of the Hunzas against the British, and many of the missiles were kept as curiosities. This use has also been mentioned in stories of Indian wars in the Southwest.

The garnet is occasionally regarded as a royal gem because it carried the image of the sovereigns of Persia. As an amulet, it was very much favored by travelers, for it was said to protect and preserve honor and health, cure the wearer of all diseases, and guard him against perils during a journey. All these powers were said to double for people born in January.

The garnet is the fourth stone in Aaron's breastplate, and its ruddy warmth and brightness are so great that Noah was supposed to have lighted his ark with its light. Christian tradition considered the blood-red garnet symbolic of Christ's sacrifice, and in the Koran it illuminates the fourth heaven. The Egyptians wore garnets as talismans, too, and the Aztecs offered them as tributes to the gods. The Greeks, as long ago as 300 B.C., were the first to use garnets as signet rings.

Because the color of the garnet has long been associated with blood, it was considered an incomparable cure for all disorders of the blood. Since anger causes the face to flush, the garnet was used as a charm against the effects of anger and was said to be a calming influence and even a remedy for mental disorders. Soldiers in combat wore garnets for protection against battle wounds.

The most expensive garnet is the brilliant green variety, called demantoid (diamondlike), which approaches emerald shade and exceeds the diamond in fire, or dispersion. The finest of these garnets, which are quite rare, are found in the Ural Mountains.

Like other gems, the garnet was once believed to guard the wearer against poisons and bad dreams. More recently it has been credited with bringing the wearer loyalty, success, and popularity. To dream of garnets meant wealth in one's future.

The garnet is quite durable, and many pieces of antique garnet jewelry are still being worn today. Its long history and durability seem to confirm its promise of constancy as the birthstone for January. The garnet is available in natural stones, grossular or synthetic garnet-colored corundum.

FEBRUARY: THE AMETHYST

Amethyst, the most valuable crystal of the quartz family, comes in many colors, ranging from pale, delicate lilac to rich, deep purple. It derives its name from a Greek word meaning "not intoxicated" and has been known historically for its ability to help one maintain that condition.

According to ancient myth, Bacchus, the god of wine, was so enraged over a slight by the goddess Diana that he vowed that the first person to enter his forest would be devoured by his tigers. This luckless mortal turned out to be the beautiful virgin Amethyst, who was on her way to worship at the shrine of Diana. As the ferocious beasts sprang on her, she called on Diana for help and was turned into pure white stone. In repentance for his cruelty, Bacchus poured the juice of grapes over the stone and gave it its purplish-violet color. In memory of the transformed nymph, the stone that bears her name was endowed with the power to protect the wearer from the evils of intoxicating drink. It later became the custom to drink wine from cups of amethyst in order to insure that one would remain sober.

The amethyst was credited with many other extraordinary attributes. Among its reputed benefits was an ability to quicken the intelligence and make the owner more successful in business, protect the soldier and assure victory, help hunters, guard against contagious diseases, and control evil thoughts.

To men, the amethyst promised sober judgment and industry; to women, lofty thoughts and religious love.

Catherine the Great was so fond of the amethyst that she sent thousands of workers to search for the gem in the Urals; the stones they brought back were prominent among her royal jewels. Many other monarchs admired the amethyst and identified with its power; hence the expressions "royal purple" and "born to the purple." The amethyst appears in the coronation regalia of England, in the king's scepter, and in the coronet of the prince of Wales.

The amethyst, too, has had religious associations. It was among the gems in Aaron's breastplate and is worn by many bishops in the Roman Catholic Church. The bishop's ring set with an amethyst is regarded as a symbol of ecclesiastical status and is generally worn on the second finger of the right hand.

The most valued hues of amethyst range from deep purplish-red to purple-red. Deep, evenly colored specimens are particularly desirable. The principal sources of fine-quality amethyst include Brazil, Uruguay, and the Ural Mountains. Other areas of the world that have produced important quantities are Sri Lanka, Japan, Mexico, South Africa, the United States, Madagascar, and Iran.

As the birthstone for the month of February, the amethyst, which signifies sincerity, is available in natural stones or synthetic amethyst-colored corundum.

MARCH: THE AQUAMARINE AND BLOODSTONE

The aquamarine, which derives its name from a combination of words *aqua* and *mare*, meaning "sea water," has been described by the ancients as "a thousand leagues of sunlit sea imprisoned in a cup." Its color varies from deep blue to greenish-blue and is like the transparent sea itself.

Aquamarine has long been considered the symbol of happiness and everlasting youth. The Egyptians, Greeks, and Romans valued it highly, and many museums exhibit aquamarine specimens enhanced by old intaglio engraving and cameo carving. It was once the special talisman of ocean travelers, assuring them a successful voyage and safe return. It was counted on to renew married love, develop forbearance, cure laziness, and further litigation.

In the Middle Ages the aquamarine was said to bestow insight and foresight and have the power to induce sleep. He who held an aquamarine in his mouth could call a devil from hell, who would answer any questions he wished to ask. The power of the stone to fight evil enabled its wearer to conquer all wickedness. Water in which an aquamarine was soaked was believed to cure eye trouble, stoppage of breath, and hiccups.

Aquamarines were associated with the purity of the oceans and hence were credited with the power to keep its wearers clean in body and spirit. The ancients wore aquamarines engraved with the head of the sea god to protect them against the perils of the deep. In Egypt the stone is believed to have been used to invoke the aid of cunning water spirits and mighty heroes. In the ordering of the New Jerusalem, the gem was assigned to St. Thomas, the apostle, who made long journeys by sea to preach the faith.

The many other virtues and magical powers of the aquamarine include protection from enemies and poison, quickening the mind, and rendering the wearer fearless, relaxed, and amiable. The lovely color in aquamarines is caused by a minute amount of iron compound. The aquamarine is the blue variety of beryl, the same mineral as emerald. The best aquamarines have great transparency and brilliance and often come in large crystals. In 1910 an aquamarine crystal was found in Brazil that weighed 243 pounds and was so transparent that objects could be seen through its long dimension of 19 inches. The British Museum of Natural History has on display a flawless, sea-green specimen that weighs 879.5 carats, and the American Museum of Natural History has several cut specimens, including a 271-carat Russian aquamarine, a 335-carat gem from Sri Lanka, an emerald-cut 144.50-carat Brazilian stone, and another one of top quality weighing 400 carats. Experts consider the most beautiful aquamarine ever discovered to be one that came from Brazil and was once owned by that country's emperor Dom Pedro. Aquamarines are mined principally in Brazil.

In America the aquamarine was given an enormous boost in popularity in 1906 when President Theodore Roosevelt's daughter, Alice Roosevelt Longworth of "Alice Blue Gown" fame, was given a beautiful heart-shaped aquamarine by Vice President William Howard Taft as a wedding gift.

This birthstone for March is available in natural stones or synthetic spinel.

The companion birthstone for March is the bloodstone, which is mainly worn by men and is often carved with monograms, initials, or crests.

The bloodstone is said to represent the blood of Christ, a belief that has been expressed in some of the gems cut from this stone. On these the thorn-crowned head of Christ is so placed that the red spots of the bloodstone simulate drops of blood trickling down His hair and face. Such gems are especially revered as Christian amulets.

The bloodstone was once used to check hemorrhages. In the sixteenth century an Italian painter named Luca Signorelli was placing one of his paintings in a local church when he saw a man become seized with a hemorrhage attack and faint away. Without a moment's hesitation, Signorelli took a bloodstone amulet from his pocket and slipped it between the man's shoulders. The hemorrhage is reported to have stopped instantly. Certain Indians also considered the bloodstone a remedy, but they first cut it into the shape of a heart. Because of its religious significance, the bloodstone has been endowed with many other curative powers and was once used to counteract poisons.

As the March birthstone for men, the bloodstone is supposed to give its wearer courage and make him brave in the face of all danger. In addition, it is reputed to impart wisdom and an ability to detect and foil enemy plots.

APRIL: THE DIAMOND

The hardness and durability of the diamond have always stood for an eternally incorruptible principle that protects its wearer from evil. In addition, the fact that white light is composed of all colors convinced the ancients that the diamond, the gem of light akin to the sun, was a combination of all the other precious stones.

The diamond has played a part in almost every religion. In the Talmud, a gem supposed to have been the diamond was worn by the high priest and served to show the guilt or innocence of one accused of any crime. If the accused were guilty, the stone grew dim; if he were innocent, it shone more brilliantly than ever. The Hindus classified diamonds, like rubies,

according to four castes. The Brahman diamond meant power, riches, friends, and good luck; the Kshatriya diamond prevented the onset of old age; the Vaisya stone brought success; and the Sudra, all manner of good fortune. Soldiers believed that a diamond carried into battle would keep them safe from harm and even render them invisible.

The far-reaching magic of the diamond, barely touched on in previous chapters, included indomitable power against poison, fears, nightmares, sorcery, quarrels, lunacy, and possession by devils. Diamonds brought power, riches, success, friends, everlasting youth, and the promise of serenity and contentment.

Like the emerald, the diamond was reputed to be a reliable test for fidelity, and a stone placed on the breast of a sleeping lover was expected to make him tell all. Another device was to rest a diamond on a wife's head without her knowledge while she slept—a mean feat in itself! If she were faithful, she would turn to her husband in her sleep; if not, she would move away.

An old English ballad tells of the romance of a beautiful princess who, when her suitor bade her farewell and went to sea, gave him a ring set with seven diamonds as a memento. Some distance from home, he observed that the diamonds had turned pale and interpreted this to mean that she had found a new love. He hurried back just in time to prevent her marriage to another, and they lived happily ever after.

Synthetic spinel is also used for this April birthstone.

MAY: THE EMERALD

The emerald, the color of spring grass and greenery, still symbolizes faith, kindness, and goodness and the promises of nature in this verdant time of year. Even today the emerald is reminiscent of the goddess Venus and the days when lovers believed it was endowed with the power to reveal the faithfulness of one's beloved.

The emerald, in addition to its supposed benefits described in Chapter 5, was said to cure fever and epilepsy when worn around the neck. An emerald suspended so that it touched the abdomen and another emerald in the mouth were used to relieve the ravages of dysentery.

Hindu physicians of the thirteenth century considered the emerald a good laxative when ground to a powder and drunk in a liquid and said the mixture promoted bodily health. They called the emerald "cold and sweet." It was also believed that a stone placed on the ailing part of the body would send forth emanations of its therapeutic power. Probably the brilliant reflected light of these gems gave rise to the idea that they radiated a healing energy.

At the time of the Spanish conquest, an emerald the size of an ostrich egg was worshiped by the Peruvians and called the Emerald Goddess Umina. Like other precious relics, it was only displayed on high feast days, when the Indians flocked to the shrine with gifts for the goddess. The priests had suggested the donation of emeralds, saying that they were daughters of the goddess and she would be pleased with them. A huge store of emeralds was thus collected, but they were destined to fall into the hands of the Spanish conquerors. The mother emerald, however, was so cleverly hidden that the invaders never found it. Many of the pillaged emeralds were destroyed because the new owners thought the test of a real emerald was its ability to withstand the blows of a hammer. The old and entirely false myth that a genuine diamond could survive such a test may have been responsible.

The emerald has been the favorite of many historical figures. Alexander the Great had a large one set in his jeweled girdle; and emeralds were prominent among the stones in Charlemagne's crown.

The word *emerald* has been traced to many ancient languages and in each case means "green." As the birthstone for those born in May, the emerald denotes love and success. It is available in natural or synthetic varieties.

JUNE: THE PEARL, ALEXANDRITE, AND MOONSTONE

Pearls, of course, are not stones at all but are the organic products of a few types of shellfish. The pearl is the only gem that does not have to be cut and polished and is ready to wear when it is taken from the shell in which it has grown.

The Egyptians, Persians, and Hindus held the pearl in great esteem and the Romans learned of it from them. Even the couches and trappings of the Romans literally glowed with pearls, and Roman women wore them in their sleep so that the presence of the gems would always remind them of their wealth. Julius Caesar, too, was a great fancier of pearls.

The pearls brought back from the Orient by the Crusaders probably spread the appreciation of these gems to Europe, where again they were worn as personal ornaments by men and women of high rank. In fact, pearls were so much in vogue that a subsequent period in European history was called the Pearl Age.

Not only was the pearl sacred to the Greek goddess of love, Aphrodite, and to her Roman counterpart, Venus, who also came from the sea, but the white radiance of the gem made it a favorite of Diana, the chaste moon goddess. Pearls were dedicated to the Angel Gabriel and adorned the gates of the New Jerusalem, probably the original "pearly gates." They were fundamental in the Table of the Koran, and the Hindus thought them the divine creation of Vishna.

The pearl has always been the gem of modesty and purity and has been believed to have a power for the good—to bring succor in troubled times, to cement friendships, and to strengthen weak hearts and memory. The pearl supposedly gives its wearers the courage to resist and overcome evil; it eases irritability, wards off pestilence, increases the fruitfulness of oxen, and cures blood disorders.

The most beautiful pearl ever is claimed to be La Peregrina, meaning "The Wanderer," a gem with a long and color·· ful history. It was found over four hundred years ago in Panama by a Negro slave who was said to have been given his freedom for it, and then sent to King Philip II of Spain by his conquistadores in 1570. This matchless white pearl, which weighs over twenty-seven carats and is about one and one-half inches long, was given to Mary I of England and then to Prince Louis Napoleon of France, who sold it to a British marquis to raise needed cash. It disappeared for a period and in 1969 was bought by Richard Burton as a birthday gift for Elizabeth Taylor.

As the birthstone for June, the pearl brings a promise of health and longevity. It is available in natural or cultured varieties.

One alternate birthstone for June, the alexandrite, is a variety of the mineral chrysoberyl. It has the remarkable property of displaying two colors—it is green by day and red by night. Poetic writers have called it "an emerald by day and a ruby by night."

This gem derives its name from the fact that it was discovered on the birthday of Alexander II, czar of Russia, in 1839, (then heir-apparent) the year he reached his majority. The story goes that a group of miners in the Ural Mountains found some stones that looked like emeralds, but when they took them back to the camp that night, the campfire light made them shine red. In the morning, however, the stones shone green again, and the men realized that they had found a new gem. Because red and green were the imperial Russian colors, alexandrite has been a favorite of that country.

The alexandrite is rarely found in large sizes, and the 43-carat and 27.5-carat specimens of exceptional quality in the British Museum are outstanding examples. A record 60-carat alexandrite is on view at the Smithsonian Institution.

The alexandrite, regarded as an omen of good luck, is available in natural stones, and synthetic alexandrite.

An additional June birthstone is the moonstone, so named because of bluish-white internal reflections that seem to have a silvery play of color like the moon. The more of this silvery light a stone has and the more translucent it is, the greater its value. Not all moonstones have this pearl-blue hue; some have a green, blue, or yellow tint instead. When the gem is turned back and forth, it shows silver rays that have been compared to moonbeams dancing over the water.

Because it has no sharp edges, the moonstone is sometimes likened to a raindrop or tear. The Orientals, steeped in gem lore, point out that when there is a moon there is no rain and so the name, moonstone, means "no tears." The moonstone is believed to arouse tender passions in lovers. According to legend, a moonstone placed in the mouth while the moon is full gives lovers the power to read their futures together.

Moonstones have been found in Switzerland, Sri Lanka, and more recently in India. Small stones are found relatively often; larger stones of unflawed quality are more rare.

The moonstone has always been regarded as a harbinger

of luck and is held in high esteem in the Orient, where it is believed that it has a live spirit that moves as the stone is turned. Superstition says it has the power to hypnotize the person who gazes at it as it moves back and forth. In India it is regarded as sacred and can only be displayed on a cloth of yellow, since that is a sacred color. The moonstone temple, built about 1100 B.C. at Anuradhapura, Sri Lanka, had altar steps paved with moonstones. Its ruins are still visible.

As a June birthstone, the moonstone is a lucky one that stands for friendship.

JULY: THE RUBY OR STAR RUBY

The ruby has been said to surpass all other stones in virtue and value. The Hindus valued it so highly that they called it the "king of precious stones," and "the leader of precious stones," and they described one particular shade of ruby as "red as the lotus." When they classified rubies by castes according to their quality, no inferior stone was allowed to touch a superior one, lest the great powers of the better gem be diminished. They also believed that whoever gave rubies to the god Krishna was virtually certain to be reborn an emperor in a future reincarnation. The ruby meant a life of peace and health for the owner and the assurance that his land and rank would never be taken from him. His garden would be safe from storms and his future filled with good fortune.

Many men of science believed in the medicinal powers of the ruby and praised its therapeutic value. When, in 1663, English physicist Sir Robert Boyle supported this view, rubies were offered for sale by druggists as cures for various ills, and famous "ruby elixir" was created by a secret method for wealthy patients. It was placed on the tongue, which subsequently became cold and heavy, as did the fingers and toes. This was followed by violent shivering. When these effects had disappeared, the cure was considered complete. The stone was also used as a disinfectant in certain dread diseases. Even the notorious Ivan the Terrible had some kind words to say about the ruby and declared it very good for the heart, brain, and memory and an excellent blood purifier. It has even been claimed that the ruby is empowered to settle disputes and assure friendly reconciliations.

As the birthstone for July, the ruby signifies contentment. Rubies are available both natural and synthetic.

> *"And they were stronger hands than mine*
> *That digged the Ruby from the earth—*
> *More cunning brains that made it worth*
> *The large desire of a king."*
> *Rudyard Kipling*
> *From "A Dedication to 'Soldiers Three'"*

AUGUST: THE PERIDOT AND SARDONYX

Because of its great radiance, the peridot was called the "gem of the sun" by the ancients who believed it had the power to ward off darkness. The peridot is bright olive green, so brilliant that it flashes even in dim light.

The peridot was favored for earrings because of the belief that its power over light was transferable to sound and would make even the faintest sound more audible. The peridot was thought to put evil spirits to flight, drive off the terrors of the night, and endow its owner with a sane mind, a kind temperament, and persuasive eloquence. For the peridot to exert its full powers as a talisman, however, it had to be set in gold. For it to work as a defense against the wiles of evil spirits, the stone had to be pierced and strung on the hair of an ass and then attached to the left arm.

When ground into a powder, peridot was taken as a remedy for asthma, and when held under the tongue, it was supposed to lessen the thirst of a fever.

Only by night and on royal authority could a search be made for this stone. The peridot was years ago dedicated to St. Bartholomew.

Many beautiful examples of peridot were brought back from the Mediterranean area during the Crusades, by loot or by trade, and found their way into the cathedrals of Europe, where they were presented as emeralds. The peridot is sometimes called the "evening emerald."

The most important source of peridot has been the island near Egypt in the Red Sea now known as St. John's (formerly Zebirget, which is the Arabic word for peridot). It is here that the most beautiful medium-dark-green crystals are found. The mines that produced peridots were worked as early as 1500 B.C., and in those days Zebirget was known as the Isle of Serpents because it was infested with poisonous snakes that made mining operations difficult. Later a reigning Egyptian monarch had the snakes driven out so that work could proceed. The workers, who lived on the island, were forced by the king to dig for the stones and deliver them to the royal gem-cutters. Reportedly, because it was difficult to distinguish the lustrous peridots in daylight, the searchers would go out at night, mark the location of the stones, and return the next day to work the area. The monarchs valued the stones so highly and feared theft so greatly that guards were posted and ordered to kill any suspicious persons approaching the shore.

One of the finest peridot specimens formerly belonged to the Russian czars and is now in the Diamond Treasury in Moscow. It is a yellowish-green, almost flawless stone, weighing 192.75 carats, and it was once mounted in a setting with thirty diamonds. Other peridots may be viewed in the American Museum of Natural History in New York and the Field Museum of Natural History, Chicago.

As the birthstone for August, the peridot assures married happiness. It is available in natural stones or synthetic spinel.

The sardonyx, the alternate birthstone for August, was one of the stones set into the breastplate of the High Priest Aaron. It is multilayered, and its name is derived from that quality and the fact that it is a reddish-brown veined onyx. The name is used incorrectly for carnelian and, more often, for sard or carnelian onyx.

The sardonyx is known as the "gem of courage" for orators and bashful lovers and was said to be a charm against such assorted afflictions as warts, boils, cramps, the evil eye, and the wicked thoughts and impulses of witches.

Probably the most famous sardonyx was the one set in the gold ring and carved with the portrait of Elizabeth I. The Queen gave this ring to her lover, the earl of Essex, as a memento and keepsake. The sardonyx is on exhibit in many museum collections of Egyptian, Roman, and Greek stones. It was a favorite gem of the ancients, and many thousands of years ago the Egyptians engraved these gems as scarabs and beetles and wore them as talismans. Roman soldiers often wore sardonyx stones engraved with Mars, the god of war, to render them brave and fearless in battle.

The sardonyx is popular in cameos and intaglios or can be cut for crests or initials.

SEPTEMBER: THE SAPPHIRE AND STAR SAPPHIRE

The throne of celestial judgment is supposed to rest on sapphire, and one ancient writer wrote that "the figure of a ram or bearded man engraved on a sapphire has the power to cure a person from many ailments and free him from poison or demons." At the time it was believed to remove all impurities and foreign matter from the eyes. It is said that Charles IV used an oval sapphire for this purpose. In 1391 a sapphire was left at St. Paul's in London by a generous benefactor who stipulated that it should be kept at the shrine of St. Eskenwald to cure eye diseases and that a proclamation should be made of its remedial values.

Oriental tradition described the sapphire as a guiding gem, one that warded off evil omens and brought good fortune to its owner. The nineteenth-century explorer Sir Richard Burton, who translated *The Arabian Nights,* owned a large sapphire and claimed that it brought good horses and prompt service wherever he went.

Ranging from pale sky-blue to the deepest indigo, the sapphire was believed to have the power to attract divine favor. Ever since it was called the "gem of gems" by the bishop of Rennes in the twelfth century, it has been a favorite for ecclesiastical rings. The ancient Egyptians said that wearing a sapphire would make the stars move into a favorable position and that the star sapphire—a sapphire in which the crystalline structure reflects light in the form of a six-rayed star—appeared especially influential for this purpose.

Since the sapphire produced such beneficent magic, evil could not prevail in its presence. The very proximity of the stone would kill reptiles as well as venomous insects. The sapphire was long honored by necromancers because it was so superb a talisman against evil spirits, and there were those who considered it even more effective than the emerald for eye ailments. When King Solomon adopted the sapphire for his seal, the stone became even more of a symbol of wisdom and clear thinking.

As the birthstone for September, the sapphire still signifies clear thinking. It is available natural or in synthetic form.

OCTOBER: THE OPAL AND TOURMALINE

The opal is considered by many to be the most beautiful and desirable of all gems, for it is highlighted with all the colors of the rainbow. White or black opals combine many colors.

According to legend, the wearer of an opal will be urbane and courteous and protected from the wrath of others. The stone was also reputed to make its owner invisible to foes and thereby exempt from misfortune. Opals were supposed to drive away despondency and evil thoughts, cure kidney diseases and cholera, soothe the eyes and nerves, and protect against lightning. It made wishes come true and was particularly favorable to children, the theater, amusements, friendships, and emotions. It is the gem of inspiration in the arts and in love.

The opal was regarded as a means to clairvoyance, one far more effective than the traditional crystal ball. A famous European telepath testified to his unshakable belief in the powers of the opal by declaring, "Anyone could do what I do if he had my opal!"

The word *opal* is derived from the Latin *opulus* and the Sanskrit *upala,* meaning "precious stone," and was one of those in the breastplate of Aaron. It was the lucky stone of the Romans, who called it *cupid paederos,* which meant "child beautiful as love," and who revered it as the symbol of hope and purity.

Pliny described the opal as possessing "the fire of the carbuncle, the brilliant purple of the amethyst, and the sea-green color of the emerald, all shining together in incredible union." The Arabs believed that opals fell from heaven in flashes of lightning and thus acquired their colors. In ancient Greece opals were supposed to confer foresight and prophecy on their owners.

Black opal has been regarded as an exceptionally lucky stone and in early times was made artificially by dipping light-colored stones into ink or by allowing burned oil to enter cracks produced by heating.

Blondes have always had a special fondness for opal necklaces, which were supposed to guard the color of their hair.

Sometimes bad luck and good luck appear to be dual effects of the opal. The story is told of a Paris shopgirl who was crossing a street during heavy traffic and stopped at a safety island for a few moments. An elegantly dressed lady slipped a magnificent opal ring from her finger and without a word gave it to the surprised girl. When the girl tried to sell it to a jeweler, she was arrested on suspicion of having stolen the ring. The presiding judge was inclined to believe her strange story and asked the newspapers to urge the lady who gave the girl the ring to come forward and clear her. Happily, the lady did so, explaining that she feared bad luck from possession of the ring and had therefore given it away. Because the ring had brought her such good luck, the girl kept it and wore it with pride.

Opals have been worn by many well-known figures. Queen Victoria was especially proud of her opal collection, and gave each of her five daughters a magnificent opal as a memento. Sarah Bernhardt, the famous French actress, whose birthstone was the opal, never considered herself well dressed without her opal jewelry and added enormously to its popularity. As mentioned earlier, the Roman senator Nonius chose exile rather than sell his beloved opal ring to Mark Antony; the ring was found in Nonius' tomb.

Among the most famous specimens of opal are the Devonshire opal, a magnificent black stone from Australia that weighs about 100 carats. Many other well-known opals of fine quality have been found in Australia. The Roebling opal, a 2,610-carat gem from Nevada, is one of the largest known and is exhibited at the Smithsonian Institution. Another Nevada opal on display at the Smithsonian is a 355.19-carat cabochon-cut black opal.

As the birthstone for October, the opal stands for hope and is available in natural or synthetic stones.

Although tourmaline, the alternate birthstone for October, was probably known to the ancients and must have been present in many of the Oriental mines yielding precious stones, there are no descriptions of it by early writers that we can consider definite.

During the seventeenth century, dark green tourmaline crystals shipped to Europe from Brazil were called Brazilian emeralds and incorrectly credited with a hardness greater than that of true emeralds. However, early in the eighteenth century it was discovered that these crystals had a unique property. One warm summer day, while some Dutch children were playing with stones that had been brought home by navigators, they noticed that the stones attracted small bits of ash and pieces of paper. The children's parents, summoned to view the phenomenon, were astounded at the magnetic properties of these stones, which were later given the name, *aschentreckers*, meaning ''ash drawers.''

The word *tourmaline* however, is derived from the ancient Singhalese word *tormall*, meaning ''mixed precious stones.'' It is a complex silicate combined with various metallic elements; since each contributes a different color, the observer is often confused into believing the gem is a ruby, emerald, or sapphire.

The most valuable variety of tourmaline is red to purplish-red to violet-red. It comes in an infinite variety of hues and tones. Most common are green and light red tourmalines, but others are dual-colored stones in blue, yellow and pink, brown and black. Some stones show several colors; they may be one color at the base, another at the center, and a third near the apex. In others, the interior portion will be one color and the peripheral zone another. When the central portion is pink and the periphery green, the resulting combination is called a ''watermelon'' tourmaline. Cat's-eye tourmalines also are found in a variety of colors.

Brazil is still the most important source of tourmaline, but recently California has become a significant producer of the stone. Other sources include Madagascar, Maine, Sri Lanka, Burma, and Russia.

Tourmaline may be cut into any style, including step, brilliant, mixed, and cabochon. It is often carved into flowers, leaves, and similar forms and set in jewelry with diamonds and other colored stones. The 173-carat tourmaline in the Smithsonian Institution is regarded as the finest example of the tourmaline.

Tourmalines are available in natural stones or in synthetic pink corundum.

NOVEMBER: THE TOPAZ

The topaz comes in many colors, but the yellow variety, discovered in the Middle Ages during a quest for a supreme golden stone, is the most familiar. At one time, all yellow-colored stones were called topaz.

In Oscar Wilde's *Salome*, Herod tries to persuade Salome to withdraw her request for the head of John the Baptist by offering her great riches. Among the treasures he describes are "topazes as yellow as the eyes of tigers, topazes as pink as the eyes of wood pigeons." In addition to the varieties Herod offered are blue, brown, red, and colorless topazes.

The name *topaz* is derivative of the Sanskrit word *topas*, meaning "fire." When worn as an amulet, it was said to drive away sadness, strengthen the intellect, and bestow courage. A topaz mounted in gold and hung around the neck was believed to dispel enchantment.

The powdered stone was put in wine and used as a cure for asthma, insomnia, burns, and hemorrhage. It was regarded as the stone of fruitfulness and faithfulness, and one that conferred cheerfulness on the wearer, calmed passions, and pre-

vented bad dreams. St. Hildegard prescribed the use of a topaz to cure dimness of vision, recommending that the stone be immersed in wine for three days and three nights. The patient was advised to rub his eyes before going to sleep with the moistened topaz so that it lightly touched the eyeballs. Topaz was said to cure jaundice and other disorders of the liver and was prescribed as a sure remedy for all contagious diseases. It was empowered to counteract poison and instantly quench the heat of boiling water. All these magical powers were believed to increase and decrease with changes of the moon.

The topaz was a holy stone signifying St. Matthew, and pilgrims flocked to Rome just to touch the topaz owned by Popes Gregory II and Clement VI, which was said to cure all ailments and to bring health. This particular topaz was used by a Roman physician of the fifteenth century to cure those stricken by the plague by touching the infected sores with it.

The topaz was credited also with banishing the fear of death and insuring a peaceful demise. It gave its owner faith and charity, and symbolized true friendship, lasting love, intelligence, and beauty.

Of all the colors in which topaz is found, the violet-red stones are the most valued. The sherry topaz is so called because its color resembles that of sherry wine. Valuable topaz displays a slightly velvety texture and has a high luster. Citrine, or topaz quartz, is sometimes sold as genuine topaz, but a reputable jeweler will correctly represent it for what it is. Blue topazes are often quite beautiful, and some rare specimens are comparable in color to aquamarines and, more rarely, to sapphires. All colors except yellow and brown are light to very light in tone. Other factors being equal, the darker the tone the more valuable the stone.

Many fine specimens of large topazes are on display at the American Museum of Natural History, among them two pale blue stones weighing 308 and 120 carats respectively; two deep blue stones weighing 258 carats and 1,463 carats; a 241-carat pale orange-brown stone; and a 70-carat red one. The British Museum has a 614-carat flawless blue topaz and a colorless Brazilian one weighing 1,300 carats.

An old verse says of this November birthstone, which stands for fidelity:

> *"Who first comes to this world below*
> *With drear November's fog and snow*
> *Should prize the topaz's amber hue*
> *Emblem of friends and lovers true."*

DECEMBER: THE TURQUOISE AND ZIRCON

When the tomb of Queen Zer, the Egyptian monarch, was excavated in 1900, the mummy was found adorned by four bracelets made of turquoise and cast gold that had encircled the dead queen's arm for about 7,500 years. These bracelets are the world's oldest known pieces of jewelry and remain as beautiful today as when new.

The name *turquoise* is believed to have been derived from the French use of *pierre turquois*, meaning "Turkish stone," probably because the stone first reached Europe by way of Turkey. The Persians called turquoise *ferozah* for "victorious," and in Tibet it was known as *gyu*, which resembled the Chinese name for jade, China's most precious gem.

The history and romance of turquoise include a multitude of legends and superstitions. Most ancient civilizations— the Aztecs, Incas, Egyptians, Persians, and American Indians of the Southwest—valued turquoise very highly. In fact, the American Indians used turquoise in the sixteenth century as a medium of exchange and an adornment of their house fronts, their graves, and their persons. To them, turquoise embodied the spirits of the sea and the sky; they also believed that it had the power to bring abundant spoils to their warriors, many animals to the hunter, and happiness and good fortune to all who wore it. The turquoise was expected to protect the wearer from injury by falling, especially from a horse, and to make his steed more sure-footed. A belief still prevalent among the Navahos is that a piece of turquoise thrown into a river while saying a prayer to the rain god will almost surely bring immediate rain.

The oldest known piece of turquoise jewelry made by these early Indians was found in Death Canyon, Arizona. It was a pendant bearing a mosaic formed of eighty-one pieces of turquoise affixed to the wood with gum. Every Navaho wears a piece of turquoise, and the higher his position in tribal society the finer the stone. Few religious rites of the Indians of New Mexico and Arizona take place without the inclusion of turquoise, and almost all the Indian jewelry in the southwestern United States contains turquoise.

Great chiefs and monarchs of the past were often buried with a treasure of turquoise to guide them safely into the spirit world. This practice of the ancient Egyptians extended to the Aztecs of Mexico. Turquoise was used also as a powerful charm to protect the newborn in the voyage of life. In India it was believed that the man who looked long at the new moon and then instantly fixed his eyes on a turquoise would be assured of great wealth.

The oldest turquoise mines in the world are located on the Sinai Peninsula, and it was from this area that the Egyptians, as long ago as 5500 B.C., obtained the turquoise they used for personal adornment; beads found in prehistoric caves confirm this. By the time of the first dynasty, about 3200 B.C., the kings of Egypt were sending mining expeditions to Sinai. These ventures were highly organized and often included several thousand laborers and a military escort. The long journeys usually began in November and ended in May, before the summer heat became too oppressive. The mines were worked in this way for about two thousand years, but the turquoise they yielded was never of great quantity.

Most of today's turquoise comes from the United States, mostly from the Southwest. Arizona, Nevada, New Mexico, Colorado, and California have substantial deposits of turquoise.

The finest quality stones are an intense medium blue, with the color smooth and evenly distributed. Iran still produces some stones of this quality. The term "spiderweb turquoise" indicates a specimen with a smooth color but with a rather evenly distributed network of very fine lines.

As the birthstone for December, the turquoise promises prosperity and is available in natural or synthetic stones.

Zircon, the alternate birthstone for December, comes in a wide variety of colors—brown, brownish-red, red, gray and yellow, green, and orange. Natural colorless stones as well as heat-treated colorless ones have been known for years, and more than one hundred years ago colorless zircons were mentioned as possible substitutes for diamond. The huge "diamonds" that decorated the harnesses of ceremonial elephants in Oriental pageants were doubtless zircons.

Blue and colorless stones occur naturally but are not found in sufficient quantity or quality for commercial use. It was not until the twenties that this gem mineral became popular. Material discovered in what is now Cambodia was found to change to blue when heat-treated. Similar material was discovered later in Thailand. For at least four hundred years, the colorless stones had been known as Matara diamonds, from a district of that name in Sri Lanka. When the heat-treated blue stones were first cut and put on the market, they became very popular.

It is believed that the name *zircon* comes from the Persian *zargun*, meaning "gold colored." The natural crystals are often that shade. Hyacinth, used to describe the reddish-brown natural crystal, is derived from the name of Hyacinthus, the youth in Greek mythology who was accidentally killed by a discus and from whose blood the wild hyacinth flower supposedly sprang. During the Middle Ages, hyacinth was believed to induce sleep; promote riches, honor, and wisdom; and drive away evil spirits and plagues as well.

Certain beach sands (principally in Florida and Australia) contain a significant proportion of zircon grains. The most important types of zircon come from Cambodia and Thailand, with colors ranging from pale yellow-brown to deep red-brown. It is when they are treated that colorless, blue, golden-yellow stones are produced. Some stones are subjected to strong sunlight after cutting to bring about the color change. The cuts for zircon are very much like those for the diamond; the most successful is the round cut because it brings out a stone's brilliance and fire.

The largest blue zircon is a dark, slightly greenish-blue brilliant weighing just over 208 carats, on display at the American Museum of Natural History. Several other zircons are exhibited there, including a brown stone weighing more than a hundred carats.

The zircon is said to cheer the heart and make its wearer a winner in all enterprises. It is available in natural stones or synthetic spinel.

More about Jewelry Materials

*I*n addition to the stones discussed thus far, the following stones and materials are popular in jewelry: amber, coral, ivory, jet, jade, lapis lazuli, and cat's-eye. These and other stones are discussed in this chapter.

AMBER

Amber, one of the first materials used by man for decoration, has long been believed to have strong medicinal powers, particularly for the alleviation of goiter. This belief may have been based on amber's unusual electrical qualities and its capacity for electrification by friction. In fact, the Greek name for amber was *elektron*, the word from which "electricity" was derived.

The Greeks had the romantic idea that amber was solidified sunshine that floated in the sea, the result of pieces of the sun broken off as it sank into the water. The most ancient trading involved amber, and the purpose of some early Phoenician voyages was to bring it back from the Baltic Sea. The Romans valued amber so highly that even a small figure carved from it was said to bring in exchange more than a healthy slave. Roman women often carried a small piece of amber cupped in their hands because of its delicate aroma when warmed in this manner. Many artistic creations of amber were developed by European craftsmen; boxes and bottles, often carved from a single chunk of amber, were studded with gold or silver filigree and precious stones.

Amber, which is not a mineral but an organic product, is actually a fossilized resin of ancient trees. Specimens of amber sometimes contain the fossilized forms of insects that were caught and engulfed in the sap.

The colors of amber range from pale yellow to dark brown and even red; it may also be whitish, greenish, bluish, or of a violet cast. The major source of amber is the southern shores of the Baltic Sea in Poland. It is also found in marine deposits in East Germany, Sicily, Burma, and Romania. In the area of the Polish deposits there once stood luxurious forests containing species of pines and cypress that have long been extinct.

Amber is admired for its beauty and light weight when worn as a necklace and is most preferred in the transparent varieties. It is used in brooches, pendants, earrings, necklaces, bracelets, rings, beads, rosaries, and carved ornamental objects.

CAT'S-EYE

Cat's-eye, the best known variety of chrysoberyl, (which means "golden beryl") is one of the most interesting of all gems, with its silky luster and sharp "eye."

Assyrians dedicated the stone to their god Belus and it was therefore called *oculus Beli*, "the eye of Belus." It has always been considered an extremely lucky stone. It was and is still regarded by some Oriental nations as a sacred stone and used as a charm against witchcraft. Cat's-eye is regarded in the Orient as a preserver of good fortune and is believed to guard the owner's health and protect him from poverty. At one time it was carved in the shape of an animal's head to emphasize its unusual characteristics, and the natives of Ceylon regarded it as a potent charm against evil spirits.

British royalty long favored the cat's-eye as a gem for engagement rings. The American Museum of Natural History has a superb specimen that weighs 47.8 carats, and a few have been found in sizes over 100 carats.

The optical properties of the stone, called chatoyancy, reproduce the appearance of the narrowed pupil in the eye of a cat. Chatoyancy occurs in any color of chrysoberyl, but the most valuable is slightly greenish-yellow or brownish-yellow, a color similar to that of honey. Brown, green, and yellow cat's-eye are also found. The chatoyant band is produced by the reflection of light from needlelike crystals or minute hollow tubes arranged parallel to one another in a cabochon-cut stone.

When a high quality cat's-eye is held toward a concentrated light source with the chatoyant band at right angles to the light, the half of the stone closest to the light will show the body color and the other half will appear milky. If the stone has a honey-colored body, the resulting appearance can best be described as a "milk and honey" effect.

Another interesting effect on a fine stone is the opening and closing of the eye in the presence of two overhead light sources. As the stone is revolved, the eye separates into two rays divided by a clear area and then comes together to form a single chatoyant band. One of the most unusual of all gemstones is the rare cat's-eye alexandrite that displays a tendency to strong color change similar to that of alexandrite. The combination of the two phenomena is striking.

Cat's-eyes are always cut in the cabochon shape with the rare exception of the carved stone. Whatever the color of the stone, it is important that the eye contrast sharply with the background color. Judgment of a quality stone is based on color, the position of the eye—which should be straight and thin and follow the crest of the cabochon exactly when the light source is directly over the stone—transparency, and the shape of the stone.

CORAL

Coral, a gem material of organic origin, has long been the inspiration for superstitions. It was important to the ancients for its beauty as well as its many medical uses. When ground to a fine powder and mixed with water or wine, coral was believed to cure a wide assortment of afflictions. In addition, it was thought to have the power to ward off evil, impart wisdom, staunch the flow of blood, and alleviate fever.

The Romans hung branches of coral around children's necks to guard them against danger. The faith in the power of coral as a charm continued through medieval times, and even in this century it is worn in Italy to ward off the "evil eye" and by women as a cure for sterility. Early historians reported that coral quieted the waves of the sea and protected the wearer from lightning and tornados. At the height of Roman civilization many of the citizens firmly believed that a dog collar set with coral and flint was positive protection against hydrophobia. A red liquid obtained from heating a branch of coral was prescribed as an excellent tonic that could rid the body of whatever ailed it. To retain the remarkable powers of the coral as an amulet, it was stipulated by early superstition that the coral must not be carved or otherwise worked and that it be worn in a conspicuous place; once broken, the coral lost its magic powers.

Coral, a product of warm seas, is found throughout the world in tropical and subtropical waters. The principal traditional source is the Mediterranean Sea along the coasts of Tunis, Algeria, Morocco, Sardinia, and many parts of Italy. Japan is a more recent source. Coral usually grows in shallow water, and the color of the coral seems to lighten with the depth.

Coral has a vitreous, or glassy, luster, and its value varies according to its color and size. People who work with coral can distinguish at least a hundred tones of red alone. For many years dark red was the most desired but recently pale tints have come into vogue. The possibilities of using coral as an accent or contrast are virtually unlimited. When combined with turquoise, it is particularly attractive for wear with pastel tints. Pink coral is generally flattering to blondes, and deep red and white to brunettes.

Coral is most often fashioned into beads, either round or egg-shaped, and used in necklaces, rosaries, and bracelets. Carved ornaments of coral—including cameos, intaglios, and figurines—are often fine examples of craftsmanship and creativity.

IVORY

Ivory has been used ornamentally since earliest times. Ivory carvings have been found in the mounds and ruins of cities mentioned in the Bible, and examples of these carvings from early Assyrian and Egyptian dynasties may be seen in many museums.

The whiteness, warmth, and purity of ivory made it especially appropriate as a distinctive ornament of royalty, and it was often the symbol of powerful monarchy. The Bible describes the great ivory throne overlaid with pure gold that was made for King Solomon. The "tower of ivory" and "ivory overlaid with sapphires" from the Song of Solomon are part of the litany of the Catholic Church.

The word ivory originated with the Latin *eboreus* and came to us through the old French *yvoire*. The term *ivory* usually refers to the material of elephant tusks. The composition of ivory is essentially the same as the hard, bony substance of which most teeth are composed. It is very dense and its pores are close and compact and filled with an oily or waxy solution that contributes to its polish.

Ivory, which varies from translucent to opaque, is produced by African and Asian elephants. The former are the source of the finest and most beautiful ivory, called green ivory, while the latter yield the very white Ceylonese ivory. The most valued ivory is a pale, rosy white.

JET

The lustrous, opaque black material called jet has been found in Paleolithic cave deposits and among the archeological treasures of the Pueblo Indians. During the Roman occupation of Britain and up to the present, jet has had various appeals but found its widest use as mourning jewelry in the middle of the nineteenth century.

Jet, a variety of brown coal known as lignite, is formed as the result of the compaction of driftwood that sank to the sea bottom and became embedded in fine-grained mud, which was later transformed into a hard shale rock known as "jet rock." Thus, jet is of organic origin. It has been found in this kind of shale formation in the vicinity of Whitby in England, Spain, Germany, Canada, France, and Colorado.

Jet has a nearly vitreous luster on polished surfaces and is used in beads, pendants, bracelets, brooches, rosaries, and other jewelry. The value of jet depends on its purity of color, its freedom from particles of other minerals, and its lack of fine cracks. The more compact, dense, and hard types are the most desirable, and the polish should be bright.

JADE

Jade has been treasured for thousands of years for its beauty and durability. The Chinese use the same word to describe both jade and precious stone and regard jade as the "jewel of heaven." The word *jade* comes from the Spanish *piedra de ijada*, meaning "colic stone," because the Spaniards believed it relieved kidney ailments.

Jade is a tough, hard stone, and primitive men used it before the discovery of harder metals to make axes, hammers, knives, and other tools. Later it was used for bowls, decorative carvings, jewelry, and amulets to protect against evil and to bring good luck.

The early Chinese and the people of Central America often buried their dead with jade objects. In China a piece of jade was frequently placed under the tongue, and it was believed that powdered jade drunk before death would prevent decomposition of the body. The wealthy considered an occasional bit of powdered jade to be a good tonic, and some of them swallowed jade in order to live a thousand years, become invisible, or fly through the air.

Since jade was reputed to bring good fortune, the Eskimos often carried it when fishing or hunting. In the South Pacific the inhabitants of certain islands willingly traded their daughters for necklaces of jade beads.

Jade is so tough that it is very difficult to carve, and even steel chisels will not work it. Instead, gritty materials are rubbed over the surface until it wears away. Carvers of jade must have great skill and patience, for a simple vase can take two to three years of hard work.

Carved jade pieces from Mexico date back to 1500 B.C. The early inhabitants of Central America used some jade in tools, but it was mostly used for religious ceremonies. The Aztecs considered jade to be worth many times its weight in gold and gave it to the Spanish conquerors as gifts.

The Chinese have been making jade objects for three thousand years. Even the earliest designs, dating to the eleventh century B.C., were decorated with stylized geometric patterns. Many symbols, including the popular dragon, were carved of jade and reflected the ideas of Taoism and Buddhism.

During the time of Confucius in the sixth century B.C., there had already been a long tradition of love and reverence for jade. Its color, feel and sound were widely regarded as proofs of its interior nobility. *Yü*, the Chinese character for jade, was a synonym for beauty, physical as well as spiritual. A beautiful young woman was a woman of jade; a handsome man had a countenance of jade; and the highest Taoist divinity was called the Jade Emperor.

Great reverence for jade, both as an article of personal adornment and as an object of art, is so firmly ingrained in Chinese culture that when Tz'u-hsi, the last empress dowager of China, was forced to flee in 1912 during the Boxer Rebellion she valued her jade beyond all her other jewels. She rejected a fabulous diamond tiara offered by a seeker of favor but welcomed a visitor whose gift was a small but exquisite article made of imperial green jade. It is said that during her reign, and even before, it had been the custom of jade dealers to submit their finest jade to the imperial court for consideration. Since the court invariably chose the finest translucent jade available, the term *imperial jade* became synonymous with this quality.

So much did the Chinese admire jade that those who could afford it always carried small pieces with them. They believed that some of its secret virtue rubs off when it is fingered. In addition, jade makes a pleasant musical tone when struck, a sound called by the Chinese the "voice of the loved one."

Jade can be either jadeite or nephrite. These two materials look very much alike and only an expert can tell them apart. Jadeite is slightly harder than nephrite, has a translucent glow, and comes in more colors.

Jadeite and nephrite come in many qualities and colors, including gray-green, white, grayish-white with streaks of dark green, yellow, red, brown, reddish-brown, black, and even blue or mauve. However, the substance most valued in Western countries is green jadeite. When this color occurs in a highly translucent stone, its value is exceptionally high.

The terms *imperial jade*, *gem jade*, and *emerald jade* are frequently used to describe jadeite that is intense emerald green and semitransparent, characteristics that are universally preferred. Many people consider apple green to be the finest jade. Personal preferences account for the lack of agreement, but the finest qualities still are extremely rare.

Most jade is mottled and streaked. The color of fine jade has been described by some as "penetrating," since it seems to be visible for greater distances when worn than similar green colors in other gems.

The most important factors in jade quality are its color, translucency, and evenness of color, Color is the key factor. If the piece has an intense, evenly distributed, pure green color and is semitransparent, it has the highest value. Because of the value and popularity of jade, jadelike imitations have been developed. It is therefore best to seek the services of a reliable jeweler when buying jade.

Jade comes from such widely scattered areas as Burma, Central Asia, Guatemala, Siberia, Japan, California, Alaska, and Wyoming.

LAPIS LAZULI

In earlier civilizations the lovely blue lapis lazuli shared with turquoise the distinction of being among the most prized of all gemstones. Descriptions by Pliny and other historians leave little doubt that lapis was the sapphire of the ancients. In Afghanistan are some mines that are six thousand years old. These could very well be the world's oldest mines that are still being worked.

Lapis was revered in both Egypt and Babylonia and was believed to be a cure for melancholy and for a certain fever of the time that returned every third day. Powdered lapis was also used as a tonic. The Egyptian high priest wore a lapis image of Mat, the goddess of truth, around his neck; and the gem was often mentioned as being among the treasures captured from vanquished nations.

From the time of ancient Greece and Rome through the Renaissance, lapis was pulverized to make an intense blue pigment used in oil paintings; and the monks of the Middle Ages used it in a mixture to illuminate their manuscripts. The Chinese called lapis "dark blue gold stone"; they ground it into a cosmetic for painting their eyebrows and made sheets of it into screens studded with pearls.

Lapis, which is actually a *rock* rather than a *mineral*, is opaque to semitranslucent and is usually violetish-blue in color. Sometimes it is almost bluish-violet, but blue usually predominates. Lapis is a popular stone for men's jewelry and is often used in cuff links, rings, tie clips, and other items.

OTHER GEMSTONES

Among the less common but often beautiful stones are the following:

Agate. One of the many varieties of chalcedony, agate is a microscopically crystalline form of quartz found in transparent to translucent masses. Known best in its curved, banded form, agate also comes in straight, parallel bands in a variety called onyx. In its translucent form with inclusions of any color arranged to resemble moss, fern, or tree-like patterns, it is known as moss agate. These agates vary in hues, the Indian moss agate being green. Agates are found in virtually all colors, usually of low intensity.

Amazonite. Amazonite is a green or bluish-green, opaque to semitranslucent gem variety of microline feldspar. It is also called Amazon stone. Sources include Russia, Colorado, and Virginia.

Aventurine. The name aventurine refers to a number of different stones. Used in regard to quartz, it refers to a green variety of quartzite that contains flecks of green mica. Aventurine feldspars, such as sunstone, contain flakes of hematite, which reflect light when in certain positions.

Carnelian. The first stone in the breastplate of Aaron was the sardius, an ancient name for carnelian. Its color varies from deep reddish-brown to yellow or cream-colored. More than any other people, the Moslems revered the carnelian and called it the Mecca stone. Carnelian is found in many parts of the world. The name is derived from the Latin and means "flesh-colored." These transparent stones are found in South America and Japan, but the most famous have come from India.

Chrysoprase. Chrysoprase is a pale yellow-green variety of chalcedony that derives its color from a small percentage of hydrous nickel silicate. It is translucent and ranges in color from intense yellow-green to green.

Malachite. Malachite is an opaque, bright green, ornamental, and decorative mineral often banded in light and dark layers. It is an important ore of copper, and its sources include Arizona, Africa, and Russia.

Morganite. Morganite is a pink and purple beryl named in honor of J. P. Morgan by the noted gemologist George F. Kunz. It is found in California, Brazil, and Madagascar.

Onyx. Onyx is the same as banded agate except that the alternately colored bands of onyx are always straight and parallel rather than curved. The most common kinds are black and white or gray. A stone banded only with various tones of gray or gray and white is known as onyx agate. As most commonly used, the term *onyx* generally means black chalcedony.

Rhodolite. Rhodolite is a rare, brilliant, transparent, purplish-violet type of garnet that represents a combination of almandite and pyrope. It is found in Sri Lanka, North Carolina, and Tanzania.

Smoky Quartz. A variety of transparent crystalline quartz, smoky quartz is also called cairngorm. Its color varies from smoky-yellow to grayish-brown to black. Sources include Scotland, Sri Lanka, Spain, Switzerland, Maine, New Hampshire, and Colorado.

Spinel. Spinel is a magnesium aluminate that is found in a wide variety of colors, including red, orange, blue, violet, and black. The red spinel has often been confused with the ruby, and the blue spinel with the sapphire. Spinel does not possess the variation and blend of color of the ruby or sapphire. It has a vitreous luster and is transparent to opaque.

Tiger's-eye. Tiger's-eye is a yellow or yellowish-brown ornamental and gem variety of quartz. When it has been cut with a flat surface parallel to the fibers, a changeable silky sheen is seen as the stone is turned. It is a popular stone for cameos and intaglios. When cut cabochon with the base parallel to the fibers, a cat's-eye effect is produced.

Tanzanite. Tanzanite was found in 1967 in Tanzania, Africa, when a prospector was seeking a deposit of rubies. He took a wrong turn and came upon a Masai village where the natives showed him stones he thought were sapphires. The stones were soon identified by gemologists as blue zoisite and were subsequently named "tanzanite." When held to the light and rotated, the stone shows the rich blue of the sapphire, the purple of the amethyst, and a pinkish-brown that appears almost flesh-colored.

Tiger's-eye Quartz

Cat's-eye

Tanzanite

Fire Agate

Jade

Malachite statue

Coral statue

De Long St. Ruby (100.32 cts.)

Shell

Hornbill Ivory

Lapis Afghanhistan

Rings

No one knows exactly when the first ring was worn, but there is no doubt that it is the most popular piece of jewelry. Rings have been made of every material—plaited grass, bone, animal teeth, iron, gold, silver, and platinum.

RINGS IN HISTORY

In an earlier chapter we touched on the story of Prometheus, who stole the sacred fire of the gods for himself and was chained by Zeus on a high mountain. He finally broke away, taking a part of the rock with him. Zeus let him go on the condition that he wear a link of the chain that had bound him around his finger and the fragment of the rock still bound to it. Thus, the ring was to be a reminder that he was still bound to the rock. This may be the origin of the custom of tying a string around a finger to remind one of something.

Vanity has always been a leading reason for wearing rings, and the Romans, who so loved luxury, literally covered their fingers with rings. They wore all kinds and sizes of rings, and even wore different ones in summer and winter. Some of the rings were huge, set with precious stones, and often engraved with portraits of friends or ancestors or subjects of mythology or religion.

Historians believe that the first rings were of woven grass. Prehistoric man, fearing that his soul would leave his body unless it was physically bound inside him, placed plaited grass about his waist, ankles, toes, and finally his fingers. He thereby protected his soul and began as well the symbolic wearing of rings.

Rings were originally called "finger circles." The earliest rings were found in the tombs of ancient Egypt and date back to at least twelve centuries before the beginning of the Christian era. Most of these rings are of pure gold, simple in design and massive in construction. The Egyptians were firm believers in the ring as a symbol of eternity, and often their rings featured scarabs, signifying father, man, regeneration, and eternity. Because they believed in an unending life for man's spirit, it was common for them to place such rings on the fingers of the dead.

In the ancient world, rings often denoted castes or levels of society. In Rome, for instance, at first the kind of ring a man or woman was permitted to wear was prescribed by law. Originally, only senators on ambassadorial missions wore them. Later, all Roman citizens were allowed the privilege, but only those of high status were allowed the honor of gold rings. In time, the popularity of rings of all kinds reached such proportions that people wore as many as sixteen at a time. Some of these rings were made of silver, bronze, iron, glass, pottery, ivory, amber, and carnelian in addition to the traditional gold.

Love of ornamentation was not, of course, the sole purpose of rings. They have been used and worn for many practical reasons as well. The signet or seal ring, for instance, once took the place of a man's signature or authority and was binding in legal documents and business transactions; a servant could go shopping in the marketplace with such a ring and show his authority to make a purchase for his master. It may be said that these rings were actually the world's first credit cards.

Rings have also bestowed special privileges on the recipient. The most notable of these was the gold ring set with a sardonyx that Elizabeth I gave to the earl of Essex as a memento and keepsake and to guard him against harm. When some of the earl's enemies had him thrown into prison as a traitor and sentenced to death, he wanted to send the ring to the queen but did not trust his keepers. Finally, he wrapped the ring in a paper and tossed it out the window of his prison, with written instructions to bring it to one of the queen's attendants for delivery to the queen herself. Unfortunately, the attendant into whose hands it fell was the sister-in-law of one of the earl's enemies, and the ring never reached the queen. Convinced that he was too proud to ask for her help, the queen made no effort to stay his execution and grieved over his death for the rest of her life.

Rings have also been worn as tokens of one's profession, status, or rank. The procuresses of Queen Elizabeth's time were required to wear rings with death's heads on them to remind everyone of their wickedness. At one time widows wore rings on their thumbs to denote their status. In Rome an iron ring was the mark of freemen and of political figures like Julius Caesar. Those who committed a crime, however, lost the right to wear one.

The ancient Gauls and Britons used rings as currency, and the more rings one had, the richer he was. Gladiators often wore such massive rings in combat that a single blow could be fatal. Poison rings date back thousands of years and were often created so skillfully that they gave no visible sign of their ominous contents. Hannibal, for instance, was so fearful of capture by his enemies that he always carried a ring containing poison in its hollow bezel. When he realized he was about to be taken by the Romans, he opened the bezel and swallowed the poison. Demosthenes is said to have committed suicide in the same way. And, after Crassus had stolen the golden treasure from the temple of Jupiter, Capitolinius, the faithful guardian officer, is reported to have "broke the gem of his ring in his mouth and died immediately."

Cesare Borgia, to whom poisoning was a fine art, owned a ring in the shape of a lion, with claws that were actually hollow needles through which poison would flow. Before greeting his victim, he turned the ring so that the claws pointed outward. A simple handshake would thus dispose of one who was *persona non grata*. Another Borgia ring had a movable panel that would open in a split second to drop poison into the wineglass of an unsuspecting enemy.

Poison was not the only popular filling for a hollow ring. Some rings held perfume, and by a light touch the wearer could discharge a pleasant scent, much like operating an atomizer. Somehow perfume rings never attained the widespread popularity and fame of poison rings. Apparently it was more important in those days to dispatch enemies than to win friends.

Rings with sharply pointed pyramidal diamonds were

sometimes used to write messages on glass to convey romantic sentiments. Sir Walter Raleigh wrote on a windowpane, "Fain would I rise, but that I fear to fall," to which Queen Elizabeth tartly responded, "If thy heart fail thee, do not rise at all."

The charm and magic of rings have evoked a myriad of superstitions. Because rings have neither a beginning nor an end, they are timeless and eternal. Rings were believed to make the wearer eternally beautiful and young, to foretell future events, guard the traveler against unseen perils, combat the evil eye, make one invisible to enemies, defy poisons, cure diseases, insure victory in battle—in short, rings could do all things for all people.

It is said that King Solomon left his ring behind while taking a bath and that it was accidentally tossed into the sea. Without this ring he could not exercise his judicial wisdom and had to refrain from doing so for forty days until the ring was finally found in a fish that had been caught and served at his table. Another tale has it that the Emperor Charlemagne owned a ring set with a stone that had the power to attract the love of the owner to the one possessing it. When he gave the ring to his wife, all his thoughts centered on her and he was drawn irresistibly to her. Later she became extremely ill and vowed that no other woman would ever get that ring and so attract Charlemagne. As she lay on her deathbed, she removed the stone from the ring and slipped it under her tongue so that its power would die with her. Upon her death Charlemagne was inconsolable and so distraught that he could not stay away from where her body was buried. Finally, he ordered her body exhumed and discovered the stone. Once the stone was removed, the spell was broken.

Another very important ring, one of several purported to have been the ring St. Joseph gave the Virgin Mary, came to light in the 10th century. Judith, wife of Hugo, Marquis of Etruria (now Tuscany, Italy) sent her jeweler, named Ranerius to Rome to buy jewels for her. In Rome, he met and became friends with a jeweler from Jerusalem. When Ranerius left Rome, his new friend pressed on him a ring as a pledge of friendship, urging him not to refuse it as it was "the wedding ring of Joseph and the Blessed Virgin Mary." The ring, carved from a stone of green jasper, was considered of little monetary value by Ranerius, who did not even show it to Judith. Instead, he tossed it aside into a small chest of trinkets.

It is said the jeweler's young son died at the age of 10 (the number of years Ranerius had ignored the ring). En route to burial, the young lad arose in his coffin and called to his father to bring the chest of trinkets to him. Opening the box, the boy selected the jasper ring, announcing that the Virgin Mary had bade him bring it to light so it might be viewed by the religious, and venerated.

During the years that followed, the ring was said to have wrought many miracles. In 1473, the church that housed the priceless ring was destroyed, and the ring was then given to the care of the order of Franciscans of *Clusium*. (Now Chiusi in Tuscany.)

The charmed ring of Aladdin in the fabled *Arabian Nights* illustrates the magical powers imparted to a ring in fiction. In some parts of the world the loss of a ring given as a pledge of affection was believed to be an omen of bad luck. Equally unfortunate was the breaking of a wedding ring, which was considered a sign that its wearer would soon be a widow. Another superstition held that if a gold wedding ring were rubbed on a sty on an eyelid nine times it would be a sure cure.

Rings made of silver were said to be cures for fits and convulsions, and even the ring finger itself was believed to have supreme medical powers; stroked along any sore or wound, it would promptly heal the affected area. Hoof rings, made of the hooves of various animals, were often prescribed for epilepsy. Cramp rings, believed to be effective against that widespread affliction, were so common in England that they were distributed every year by the king to rich and poor, a practice that originated with the reign of Edward II (1307-27). The curative effects of the simple gold hoops were said to be derived from the royal blessings bestowed on them. Other healing rings covered the medical gamut from eye diseases to fevers and included hiccups and sneezing. Often, to expedite results, they were inscribed with the names of religious figures such as Jesus, Mary, and Joseph. Hardly an ailment existed without a corresponding healing ring, and all the afflicted needed for relief were the appropriate prayers and a firm belief in that particular ring.

Token rings were distributed by kings, queens, and nobility for use in dire emergencies of all kinds. One such ring, in the shape of a heart, was given by Queen Elizabeth to Mary, Queen of Scots. Half the ring went to Mary and the other half was kept by Elizabeth herself. When Mary was thrown into prison and faced death, she sent Elizabeth her half of the ring as a plea for help. But Elizabeth failed to observe her promise and the hapless Mary was executed. As the episode proves, token rings were often only that.

Fraternal rings date back to the days when new knights received a heraldic ring of whatever type the king decreed. These rings symbolized brotherhood and bound each knight in solemn pledge to all others. From these rings have evolved the various fraternal pins and emblems, as well as the universally popular high school class rings. Members of lodges and orders often wear rings bearing the insignia of the organization to which they belong. And from time to time young people stimulate fads for novelty rings such as peace rings, love rings, spoon rings, and so on.

Religious and ecclesiastical rings have enjoyed a special place of their own and have been worn as a mark of dignity and authority as well as a symbol of the union between the wearer and the church. The most famous of such rings is the afore-mentioned Ring of the Fisherman, the gold seal ring of the pope that bears the figure of St. Peter in a boat, fishing, and the name of the reigning pope engraved around it. On the pope's death the ring is broken and a new one made for the new pope. Bishops are also empowered to wear special rings made of gold and set with precious stones. While the sapphire was the most popular stone for many years, more recently the amethyst has been preferred, although its use is by no means mandatory. Certain orders of nuns wear simple gold rings symbolizing their espousal with Christ and the church; and some of the early Christians in Rome wore "Christian rings" with sacred emblems to denote their faith and distinguish themselves from pagans.

One romantic tradition was the use of the poesy or poetry ring. Originally these were simple bands inscribed with a sentimental thought as "A virtuous wife, a happy life," or "Forget not he who loveth thee."

An offshoot was the message ring that spelled out a word by the initial letters of the gem names. Thus, a diamond, an emerald, an amethyst, and a ruby spelled "d-e-a-r." An amusing use of this type of ring was devised in the mid-nineteenth century by the British Free Traders who wanted to get rid of the bothersome Corn Laws. They put together a ruby, an emerald, a peridot, another emerald, an amethyst, and a lapis lazuli to spread the message—*REPEAL*.

Gems have had greater significance in rings than the spelling out of messages. A letter from Pope Innocent III in 1198 to King Richard the Lion-Hearted, accompanied by a gift of four rings, each set with a different stone, read: "The verdant hue of the emerald signifies how we should believe, the celestial purity of the sapphire, how we should hope, the warm color of the garnet, how we should love, and the clear transparency of the topaz, how we should act."

Historic ceremonies such as coronations have always

CUT AND
POLISHED

FOR HIM

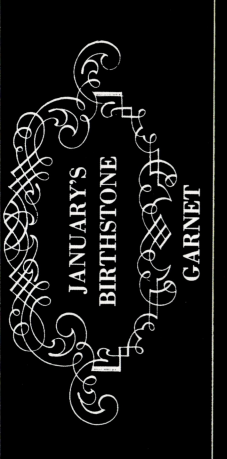

ROUGH
STONE

FOR HER

FEBRUARY'S BIRTHSTONE

AMETHYST

CUT AND POLISHED

ROUGH STONE

FOR HIM

FOR HER

MARCH'S BIRTHSTONES

AQUAMARINE / BLOODSTONE

CUT AND POLISHED

CUT AND POLISHED

FOR HIM

ROUGH STONES

ROUGH STONE

FOR HER

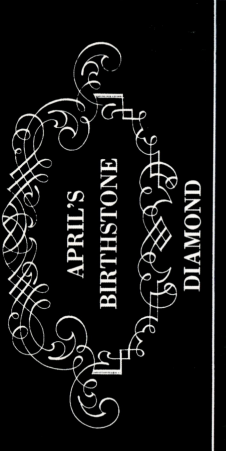

APRIL'S BIRTHSTONE

DIAMOND

CUT AND POLISHED

FOR HIM

ROUGH STONE

FOR HER

MAY'S
BIRTHSTONE

EMERALD

CUT AND
POLISHED

FOR HIM

ROUGH
STONE

FOR HER

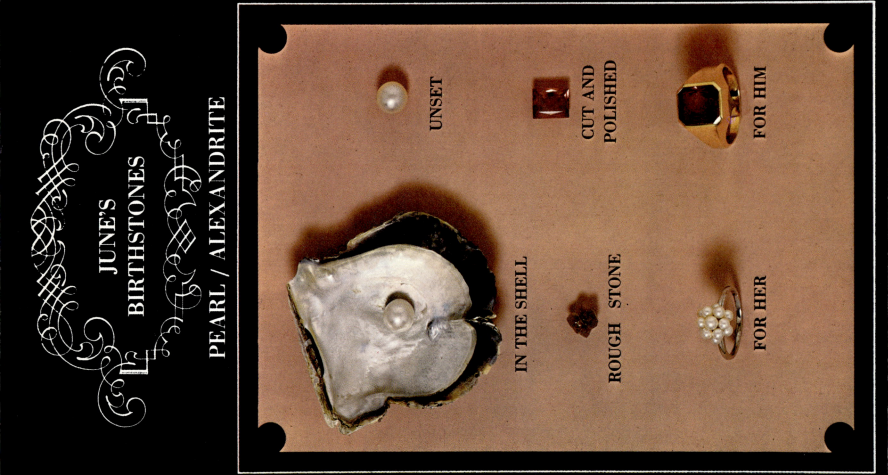

JUNE'S
BIRTHSTONES

PEARL / ALEXANDRITE

UNSET

CUT AND
POLISHED

FOR HIM

IN THE SHELL

ROUGH STONE

FOR HER

JULY'S BIRTHSTONES

RUBY / STAR RUBY

CUT AND POLISHED

FOR HIM

ROUGH STONE

FOR HER

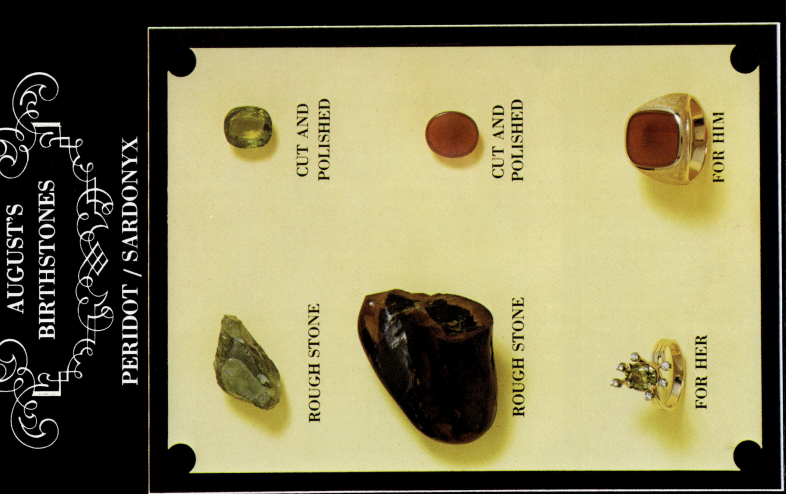

AUGUST'S BIRTHSTONES

PERIDOT / SARDONYX

CUT AND POLISHED

CUT AND POLISHED

FOR HIM

ROUGH STONE

ROUGH STONE

FOR HER

SEPTEMBER'S BIRTHSTONES

SAPPHIRE / STAR SAPPHIRE

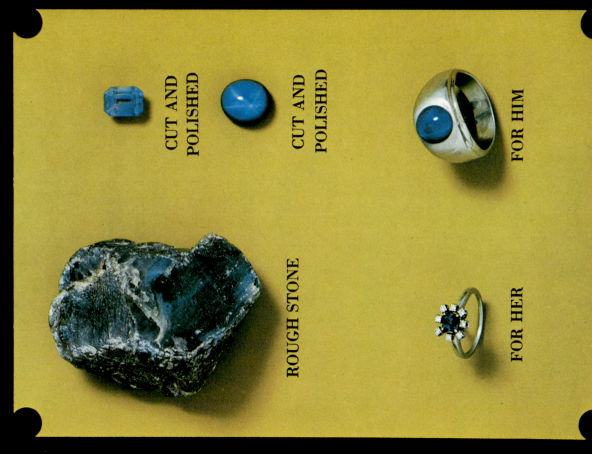

CUT AND POLISHED

CUT AND POLISHED

FOR HIM

ROUGH STONE

FOR HER

OCTOBER'S BIRTHSTONES

OPAL / TOURMALINE

CUT AND POLISHED

CUT AND POLISHED

FOR HIM

ROUGH STONE

ROUGH STONE

FOR HER

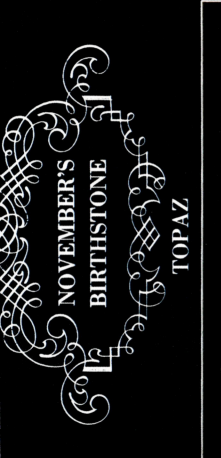

NOVEMBER'S BIRTHSTONE

TOPAZ

CUT AND POLISHED

FOR HIM

ROUGH STONES

FOR HER

CUT AND POLISHED

CUT AND POLISHED

FOR HIM

ROUGH STONE

ROUGH STONES

FOR HER

been commemorated by rings. Coronation rings symbolized the power, prestige, authority, and grandeur of the throne itself and could command obedience from all the king's subjects. The coronation ring also implied the union between the monarch and those he ruled and in England was popularly called the "wedding ring of England." In the British investiture the ring is placed on the fourth finger of the right hand of the sovereign by the archbishop of Canterbury with a special blessing. The ring is gold and set with a large ruby.

Memorial and mortuary rings were worn to mourn the death of loved ones and as symbols of affection. In some cases these rings were distributed by the dying person to friends and relatives to remind the recipients for years to come of his passing. Mary, Queen of Scots, sent memorial rings to her favorite friends before she was executed. When Charles I died on the scaffold in 1649, he urged his followers to remember him; they did so by wearing memorial rings bearing his name and portrait. Memorial rings were often specially designed with a death's head, a skeleton, or a spade and pick as reminders of the grimness of the occasion. Some of the rings had a small case or locket containing a picture or lock of hair of the deceased. George Washington left mourning rings to certain relatives and friends, and Izaak Walton made a similar provision in his will. Mourning rings sometimes carried inscriptions such as "Love my memory" or "A friend's farewell." Rings were given to attendants at funerals to mark the occasion and a special ring was given to the widow to wear in memory of her dead husband.

Rings for immoral purposes—called "rush rings"—enjoyed a vogue in the thirteenth century in England and France. They were used by unscrupulous individuals posing as clergymen to "marry" people for illicit unions of brief duration. These rings were made of straw or grass and were intended only as a cover for the bogus "marriage ceremony" of the couple seeking a sexual encounter with no moral or legal strings attached. These rush rings created such a scandal that finally they were outlawed by official decree. In the eighteenth century disreputable clergymen and others posing as clergymen performed "Fleet marriages," so named because they took place in or near the old Fleet Prison in London. These marriages were arranged without the consent of the parents of the bride, witnesses, or public notice and aroused a storm of protest when their purpose was discovered.

BETROTHAL AND WEDDING RINGS

Among the most significant rings that people exchange and wear are the wedding ring and its companion, the engagement or betrothal ring, but the origin of the use of rings as symbols of marriage is lost in antiquity. (Sources for this are Claudia DeLys "How the World Weds" and Paul Berdanier "How It Began") The cave man was said to tie his mate's wrists and ankles with braided rushes or grasses. Later only her wrists were bound and finally the rush ring was woven around her finger. Some historians report that our earliest ancestors thought that a rope tied around the body would keep the soul from escaping. Thus, when a man captured his mate, he would tie cords around her waist, wrists and ankles to keep her spirit under his control. Later a permanent ring of ivory, flint or amber was used.

It is known that wedding rings were used by the early Hebrews and by the Romans, and that these rings apparently served as both marriage and betrothal rings. The ancient Hebrews sealed the agreement of betrothal with a ring as *arrhae*, the Hebrew word for "earnest money," which represented the bridal price. To prove that a young man could afford to take a wife, he presented her with a heavy gold ring, quite massive in

Grecian wedding ring. Hexagonal shape with Greek inscription. The inscription translates "God be with you Madame. God be with you Sir. God be with him who wears you, and all his household. Remember it, Theanus is my light."

Etruscan wedding ring. Mounted with a dove.

size and beautifully decorated with filigree work and carving. This ring was too heavy and bulky for a woman to wear every day, so it was not worn until used in the actual wedding ceremony. Then it was replaced on her finger by a simple band and the original wedding ring was retained as a symbol of the couple's wedded state and prosperity. A special huge ring that was kept in the synagogue and bore a replica of King Solomon's temple with the inscription *mazel tov* ("good luck") was used in the Hebrew wedding ceremony. The Irish wedding ring, known as the Claddugh ring, bore two hands clasping a crowned heart to convey the sentiments of the occasion.

The pharaohs of Egypt were said to be the first to sketch the circle as a symbol of eternity and to believe that the ring was a heavenly sign that life, happiness, and love had no beginning or end. As time went on, various metals were used for betrothal rings. Although the early Romans wore iron rings to symbolize the permanence of marriage, by the second century gold rings were growing in popularity. Their use inspired the poet Robert Herrick to write:

> *"And as this round*
> *Is nowhere found*
> *To flaw, or else to sever,*
> *So let our love*
> *As endless prove,*
> *As pure as gold forever."*

The betrothal ring was a symbol of the bridegroom's earnestness, a pledge of his good faith, and evidence of his intention to marry. The ring the bride received at the betrothal was generally used later at the wedding ceremony. After the Reformation, the betrothal was more formal and often solemnized with the signing of the articles of marriage before witnesses.

The Romans were the first to present an engagement ring to the bride before the wedding ceremony, usually at the time the marriage contract was drawn up. The custom began with the presentation of an iron ring, and although later a gold ring was acceptable, it was worn only at the marriage ceremony and on special occasions. The Roman wife wore her iron ring at home and saved the gold one for public display. The Celts of ancient Britain developed a "love ring" that served as both wedding and betrothal ring. When a Celtic lad wooed and won a girl, he gave her a ring as a pledge of his protection. The Old English word for pledge was "wed" and this is how the name was given to our wedding rings.

Fascinating wedding rings have had their vogue through the years. In the sixteenth century the gimmal ring was popular; the word *gimmal* means "double ring," and a gimmal ring was actually two separate rings that were joined together to look like one. As a rule, a hand was engraved on each band, and when the rings were joined at the time of the wedding ceremony, the hands were clasped together. It was usual for the bride and groom each to wear half of the gimmal ring until their wedding day, when the two parts would be united on the bride's finger. If either party had a change of heart, he or she could break the engagement by withholding half. Shakespeare was referring to the gimmal ring when he wrote, ". . . a ring of pure gold she from her finger took."

In the seventeenth century romantic Englishmen gave their chosen women rings cut from the finger of the heavy gloves they wore, the highest mark of love and affection they could bestow. An ancient Hebrew betrothal ceremony called for three rings—one for the woman, one for the man she was to marry, and one for the official witness to the ceremony. The witness steered the couple to the marriage altar, where the bride donned all three rings, joined together under a signet. Some of the gold Roman wedding rings gave the wife visible

Ancient Jewish wedding ring. The projecting figure covers a small gold door which opens upon a tiny placque with the words "Mazel Tov" (good fortune). Rings of this size, much too large to wear, were for commercial use with symbolic significance.

Grecian wedding ring. Shaped in a love knot. The original of this ring, from around 1000 B.C., was found in Cyprus.

Gallo-Roman wedding ring. Dating from the 5th century A.D., the original of this ring weighs ¾ ounce. The massiveness and durability signified the perpetuity of the marriage contract.

Iron wedding ring. Has hammered effect with initials engraved on ring. Different ages and centuries employed the iron ring as it typified durability.

Saxony wedding ring. Has a flat tubular shape that twists around the finger, from ancient sepulcher at Harnham Hill, England, 7th century.

authority in her husband's household and had little knobs with keys attached to them as symbols of her power over his worldly goods.

"A ring of pure gold she from her finger took,
And just in the middle the same she then broke;
Quoth she: 'As a token of love you this take,
And this, as a pledge, I will keep for your sake.' "
(Exeter Garland)

As time went by, engagement and wedding rings became more and more elegant and beautiful. Louis IX of France, for example, gave his wife Marguerite a ring engraved with the three main loves of his life, in their priority: "God, France, Marguerite." A British marriage vow in the fourteenth century reports the groom placing the ring on his bride's finger and saying: "With this ring I thee wed and with my body I thee worship, and with my worldly chattels I thee honor."

The custom of setting wedding rings with gems began during the Middle Ages and the Renaissance, and an English will in 1503 describes a "Marying ring having dyamont." This was the wedding ring of Mary of Modina, a diamond set with gold. Jeweled rings for betrothals made their appearance in the thirteenth century.

Diamonds became popular for betrothal rings toward the end of the fifteenth century. In a letter dated July 30, 1477, to Archduke (later Emperor) Maximilian before his betrothal to Mary of Burgundy, his trusted advisor wrote: "At the betrothal Your Grace must have a ring set with a diamond and also a gold ring." The Venetians were the first to realize the possibilities of diamonds in rings and experimented with different ways of cutting diamonds to bring out "endurance and inner glow" as symbols of love. This helped establish the diamond as the preferred gem for engagement rings. Because the diamond is the hardest and most enduring substance in the world, it is as much a symbol of eternity as the ring itself.

The "keeper ring" originated in colonial times and endures to this day. It was worn during the engagement until the actual wedding ceremony at which time it was placed next to the marriage ring as a "guard ring" because of the many superstitions about the bad luck that followed the loss of one's wedding ring. In Queen Elizabeth's era it was the custom to give away remembrance rings at weddings as mementos of the occasion. These rings were of three strands of twisted wire—one for the bride, one for the groom, and one for the witness. At the wedding of Queen Victoria to Prince Albert, six dozen rings, each engraved with the queen's profile, were given to the guests.

Engaged couples sometimes would break their engagement rings in two, each keeping one half. The two pieces would be matched together on the wedding day. As with the gimmal ring, if either party changed his or her mind, the engagement could be ended by withholding that one's share.

Often rings were worn to communicate one's marital situation or intentions. If a man wanted a wife, he wore his ring on the first finger of his left hand; if he was engaged, he wore it on the second finger; if married, on the third. If his ring was on the fourth finger, it meant he never intended to get married. If a woman was not engaged, she wore a hoop or diamond ring on her first finger; if engaged, on her second; if married, on the third; and if she intended to remain unmarried, on the fourth. As a rule, a widow proclaimed her status by wearing rings on her right hand and the little finger of her left.

The betrothal or wedding ring is usually worn on the third finger of the left hand, presumably because the Greeks believed that this finger contained a vein, the vena amoris, that ran directly to the heart. While medical science does not sup-

Old French wedding ring. Octagonal in shape, it is inscribed in Old French: "It is spoken—she holds me." Dated to the 15th century.

English wedding ring. Has upside-down heart and inscription which says "God helps." Originally worn by the Episcopal priests of the Church of England, it was later used as a betrothal ring, worn on the thumb. This custom may have some connection with the old fancy that the second joint of the thumb is dedicated to the Virgin Mary.

Mary Queen of Scots and Henry, Lord Darnely's wedding ring. The ring, with its round flat face with initials engraved and name inside, was found in the ruins of Folkerngay Castle where Queen Mary was executed.

Martin Luther and Catherine von Bora. Wedding ring with sacred scenes. The original was inscribed "D Martino Luthero Catherina V. Boren 13 June 1525" and "Those Whom God has Joined Let No Man Put Asunder"

port this theory, a practical reason was it was thought that the third finger was the least vulnerable. Moreover, the English Prayer Book of 1549 specified the left hand as the proper ring hand for both bride and groom. Furthermore, the priest or minister officiating at the wedding would touch three fingers (not counting the thumb) and say, "In the name of the Father, of the Son, and of the Holy Ghost," and the ring was slipped on the last finger he touched.

There were periods in history, however, when the right hand was used. During the Middle Ages in England the wedding band was properly placed on the bride's right hand. In the sixteenth century the left hand became the rule, although English Catholics used the right hand until about 1750, as did Roman Catholics until about the same time. The practice of wearing wedding rings on the right hand is still observed by members of the Greek Orthodox Church and other religions and some ethnic groups. Arabs use the left hand but put the ring on the first finger; in India, the wedding ring is traditionally worn on the thumb.

An American bride moves her engagement ring from the left hand to the right hand before the ceremony in order to receive the wedding band. After the ceremony the engagement ring is returned to the left hand and worn outside the wedding band. Thus, the engagement ring is worn similarly to the "keeper ring," the colonial guardian of love and marriage.

The "double ring" ceremony, with a wedding ring for the bride and the groom, has been growing in popularity in the United States. The custom, well established in European countries, received great impetus when many American servicemen in World War II wore gold wedding rings while separated from their wives. More and more men wear wedding rings today.

While many brides prefer traditional designs in their wedding and engagement rings, many choose such fashion innovations as matched engagement and wedding rings and interlocking wedding bands that form a design with the engagement ring. Also available are insert wedding bands, guard rings, and circlets that may be added or subtracted as one wishes.

Although the plain gold wedding band is universally appropriate, many women choose more ornate rings, often set with diamonds. Some couples who marry in modest circumstances return to the jeweler later to replace their original choice of band or stone with a more expensive or fashionable one than the husband could afford on their wedding day.

Old customs and superstitions still play a part in weddings, usually with the objective of bringing good luck to the bride. The bridal shower, for instance, is believed to have originated in Holland. A young girl fell in love with a poor miller, but her father forbade the marriage. The miller's friends "showered" the bride-to-be with gifts so that she would be able to marry without the benefit of the traditional dowry that helped most brides set up housekeeping.

Brides have been wearing veils for centuries. Greek and Roman brides wore flame-colored ones, the early Christians wore white or purple, and Anglo-Saxon brides hid their faces behind their own hair. In some countries even today the groom meets his bride veiled and never sees her face until they are pronounced man and wife. Nelly Curtis launched the fashion for veils in this country when she wore a lengthy scarf pinned to her coiffure at her wedding to President Washington's aide, Major Lawrence Lewis. Her decision stemmed from the flattering comments her fiance had made after glimpsing her through a lace curtain at an open window.

In the old rhyme about a bride's wearing "something old, something new, something borrowed, something blue," the "something blue" is said to have been the ribbon worn on the border of the robe by the brides of Israel; in ancient times it denoted purity, fidelity, and love. Blue is associated also with the purity of the Virgin Mary. Some brides wear a lucky garter, a

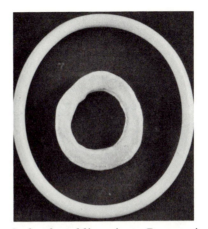

Iceland wedding rings. Bone or ivory tubular shaped, they are sometimes large enough to pass over the palm of the hand.

Indian wedding ring. Long cylinder shape said to be still in vogue today. It is worn on the thumb.

German wedding rings (gimmal ring). Consisted of two interlocking rings, joined by a pivot so that when brought together they actually constitute a single ring. These have square raised faces set with two squares of colored stones.

Early Irish wedding ring. Made of twisted gold wire.

tradition that dates back to the Noble Order of the Garter, the oldest of all orders of knighthood, whose members wear a blue velvet garter. Since only queens and noblewomen are eligible for membership, the bride wears a blue garter below her left knee to signify that she is queen for a day at least.

The bride wears white because the church has always considered white a festival color symbolic of purity. White was worn on sacred days by both Jews and the early Romans.

The flowers the bride carries are symbols of fertility and fidelity, a custom derived from the ancient Romans, who carried bunches of herbs under their wedding veils for this reason. The Saracens chose orange blossoms not only because they are considered the flowers of fertility and happiness but because the orange tree blossoms and bears fruit at the same time. Lilies have long been symbols of purity, and roses are the flowers of love. June, the month of roses, is the most popular wedding month. Ivy, first used at early Greek weddings as a token of indissoluble love, is still used to trim wedding bouquets.

The honeymoon period originated in ancient marriages. Usually the groom captured his bride and kept her hidden to prevent searching relatives from finding her. The term itself may be derived from *honeymead*, a drink early Teutonic couples drank for thirty days after their wedding or until the moon had waned. Hence, this period of seclusion has come to be known as the honeymoon.

Lifting the bride over the threshhold is a custom based on the ancient fear of evil spirits lurking at the threshhold of a new house. Thus the bride was insured protection from these spirits and any other threat to her safety. The Roman bride, usually reluctant to leave her father's house, often had to be carried into her new domicile.

All these customs and traditions—from the betrothal and wedding rings to the marriage ceremony itself—are proof, if any is needed, that the exchange of marriage pledges between a man and a woman is indeed among life's most important occasions. It is understandable that it is solemnized with offerings of value—engagement and wedding rings of precious metals and stones. While there is never any guarantee that a married couple will live happily ever after, there is always that romantic possibility, and this is the unspoken hope in every wedding ceremony.

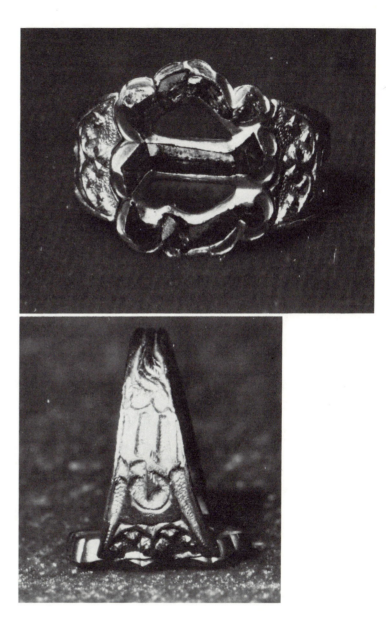

The ring Maximillian gave to Mary. Diamonds, forming the letter M, were not cut as they are today.

Jewelry for Today's Man & Woman

A gift from a king to his beloved . . ." reads a hieroglyphic inscription written more than two thousand years ago on an exquisite piece of jewelry in a fabulous Egyptian collection.

Today's woman, like those before her, still enjoys the pleasures of self-adornment, the dramatization and display of her beauty to attract, excite, and express herself. The style of jewelry a woman wears, the specific pieces she prefers, mark a woman as sophisticated, tailored, softly feminine, or free and independent. Since a woman may be any or all of these at different times, her jewelry is an extension of her personality. A woman does not simply accessorize her ensembles with earrings, pins, necklaces, rings, bracelets, and watches; she adds the personal touch that is an immediate expression of herself. Her jewelry wardrobe communicates for her and is useful as well as ornamental.

What makes it possible for the right jewelry and the right woman to meet? Quite simply, it is a basic rule—small with small and tall for tall. Proportion is all-important for the woman who wants her jewelry to complement her perfectly.

The small woman looks perfect in delicate jewelry. She can create an illusion of height with pointed necklaces, pins worn high on her shoulder, drop earrings of moderate length. Narrow bracelets are most flattering to her, and she can even wear several at a time.

The other half of the beauty mirror reflects the tall woman, who looks best in larger jewelry. Bib necklaces, wide bracelets, the mass of a corsage pin, earrings in chandelier and cluster designs—these are top form in a tall woman's jewelry collection.

Needless to say, a woman must appraise her figure and its proportions. To dress and bejewel herself most becomingly, a woman must know herself, appreciate her assets, and—bravely—acknowledge her deficiencies.

JEWELS FOR THE HAIR

Jewels for the hair are practical as well as attractive. Nearly every girl has a metal barrette (the word is from the French for "small bar") of some kind for clasping her hair. Barrettes are often made of precious metals. The Spanish comb, sometimes jeweled, is quite attractive; and the dazzling diamond tiaras of royalty have always commanded center stage and universal attention at coronations, weddings, and state occasions. But for the average woman, especially the one whose hair is beautiful in itself, a jeweled hair ornament or headband is enhancement enough.

EARRINGS

In all fashion eras, whether hair was piled high or worn loose, the earring has been prominent in the adornment of men and women. Many ancient monarchs are shown on carvings wearing earrings of all kinds. Aaron, while preparing the people to make their own gods while Moses was away receiving the Ten Commandments, said to them: "Break off the golden earrings, which are in the ears of your wives, your sons . . ."

In Rome earrings were more popular with men than with women and even Julius Caesar give this trend a strong fashion push by urging men to wear them. A portrait of Shakespeare shows him wearing one earring, and his Othello sported a gold ring in one ear. Pirates, of course, took a special fancy to the single earring and have immortalized it in their own colorful way. The English macaronis, the fops who are mocked in our song "Yankee Doodle," flaunted earrings to shock the Puritans. Charles I went to his execution wearing a drop pearl in his right ear—this seemed to end the fashion of earrings for men for a long while.

Women, however, have never wavered in their love for earrings. Huge earrings were in vogue as far back as four thousand years ago, and Queen Shubad of Sumer wore enormous golden half-moons. In ancient Phoenicia women tried to outdo one another in the size of the earrings they wore. Old Etruscan ear ornaments were made with small boxes to hold perfumes or charms. Greek prostitutes wore cupids on their ears to advertise their trade more clearly.

Queen Victoria's time saw the popularity of close-to-the-ear gold-rimmed cameos from which hung larger cameos. In Africa the fashionable Bahri matron slipped many separate elephant hairs through her ear lobes, and Zulu women stretched theirs to accommodate an ivory tube. No matter the time or the place, the earring is a universal adornment, worn everywhere with pride and pleasure.

Earrings can effect dramatic changes in a woman's appearance and set her mood instantly. Properly chosen, earrings do more to bring out her features than any other jewel, and she can perform more tricks with them than with any kind of makeup or cosmetic. They can make her appear sweetly feminine, demure, cosmopolitan, or sophisticated, and she can flit from one tempo to another in the second it takes to change.

An oval face is flattered by dangle and pendant earrings set with stones of different colors. The long, thin face needs earrings that are broad at the base but taper upward. A woman with a thin face should wear earrings as much as possible, for they add width. The round face is best framed by large, semicircular earrings, bouquets of tiny flower clusters, or pincushion and sunburst shaped earrings. The face can be lengthened by drop earrings or by earrings that are contoured to go up along the ear. A heavy chin can be minimized by upswept earrings accented with color, or by long, full dangle earrings. The effect of a too-prominent nose is softened by large earrings that do not outline the ear lobe, and sharp facial angles become softer with button or cluster earrings. To camouflage hollows under the cheekbones, large earrings should be worn close to the face.

The following suggestions are offered for the enhancement of various hair colors.

Dark Hair. Very dark stones in earrings go unnoticed

against dark hair. Better choices for the brunette are diamonds, pearls, turquoise, rubies, and coral.

Red Hair. Earrings set with brown and yellow stones should be avoided. Good color match-ups for the redhead are emeralds, jade, blue sapphire, and pink pearls.

Blonde Hair. Blondes look best in earrings set with rubies, amethysts, aquamarines, or diamonds.

Gray Hair. Diamond-set earrings are most flattering to the mature.

Earrings may be in the form of buttons, clusters, hoops, or drops. The button is a single flat or domed round; it can be a bead or it can be metal or stone. The cluster is a decorative combination of beads, stones, or metal beads. The hoop or wedding band can be in the shape of a circle that clips right onto the earlobe or dangles from a button. The drop is a loose, dangling design, often suspended from a button or cluster.

These shapes can be held to the ear by any of four types of earring backs:

1. The *screwback*, which adjusts the earring to the individual ear size.

2. The *clipback*, which has a hinge arrangement.

3. The *pierced ear wire*, which has a metal thread that goes through the pierced ear.

4. The *pierced ear screw*, which is similar to the screwback, but has a straight post that goes through the ear hole. There is also the "friction-back" type, which, instead of screwing on, is pushed on and held by a notch in the post.

A recent survey among jewelers indicated that over 80 percent of earrings sold are for pierced ears. The younger the

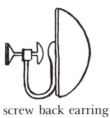

screw back earring

clip back earring

hoop earring also called wedding band earring

button earring

drop earring also called pendant or chandeleir

hoop earring

cluster earring

woman, the more likely it is that she will have pierced ears. Women feel more secure wearing pierced earrings because they will not pull or slip off like the clipbacks and screwbacks. Wearing earrings in pierced ears is very comfortable, and one is hardly aware of them. Piercing ears is a simple, quick, and painless process. For the best results, experts suggest that the ears be pierced a little high on the lobe and that karat gold studs be worn for about three weeks. After a few months, women with pierced ears can wear screwbacks, clipbacks, or any other kind of earring they like.

No two earlobes are exactly the same, and for this reason women with one earlobe larger than the other find that screwback earrings can be adjusted to fit more easily than clipbacks. Because every pair of ears and every face differs, a woman should always try earrings in front of a mirror before buying them. Pierced earrings often cannot be tried on, but they can be held to the ear for effect.

NECKLACES

Every feminine face can benefit from a fashionable and flattering necklace, the most prominent piece of jewelry of all. The lucky woman with a long, graceful neck can emphasize it with high-riding choker necklaces and strands or an unusual splash at her throat. No matter what the proportions of her neck may be, a woman can find a necklace that will do wonders for her. A short neck gains length from a long necklace, whereas a long neck will appear shorter in a choker of uniform size, beads or stones. The wide neck calls for a tapering necklace or a double-strand necklace with some noticeable space between the strands. The full neck, if it is not short as well, can be camouflaged with a necklace of large beads. Using a few simple tricks such as these, the woman who favors necklaces can easily wear them.

The necklace is a prominent adornment and should be selected with care. Poorly chosen, it can make a woman appear overdressed, and stones of the wrong color can make her skin appear sallow. The proper necklace is not only beautiful in itself but adds youth and beauty to the chinline and neck of the wearer.

The supreme necklace is the one of diamonds. The single strand—the rivière, meaning "river stream"—is a string of solitaires either uniform in size or graduated with a large center stone. The uniform rivière is often made so that it can easily be separated into two bracelets and worn for less formal occasions. Other necklaces, too—those of pearls, turquoise, coral, aquamarine, amethyst, lapis lazuli, jade, and other popular colored stones and combinations—may be selected to suit the wearer's personality and add an exciting glow to her skin. Gold necklaces in all shapes and designs are very popular, and the brightness of this metal reflects lovely highlights on the skin. Multicolored gold and varied finishes and textures can be utilized to achieve special dramatic effects. Necklaces are made flexible enough to follow the movements of the neck and may be worn with earrings and rings to mix or match. Pendants of various attractive stones and metals are quite dramatic and focus special interest on the wearer.

Necklaces are of the following types:

Collar. A collar is a flat design that fits close to the throat.

Festoon. A festoon is a short necklace with a design at the front that tapers toward the back.

Choker. Like the collar, the choker is a short necklace that fits close to the neck. It is made of bulkier materials than a collar, however.

Bib. A bib is a necklace of three or more strands.

Princess. A princess necklace is a single-strand necklace of beads, pearls, or chain about eighteen inches in length.

Matinee. The matinee is the same as the princess but about twenty to twenty-four inches in length.

Opera. The opera is a longer necklace, measuring from twenty-eight to thirty inches.

Rope. A rope is a strand that runs as long as forty-five to one hundred and twenty inches.

Lariat. A lariat is an open-ended long strand necklace.

Pendant or Lavaliere. A pendant or lavaliere is a drop, locket, or similar design suspended on a single chain.

PINS AND BROOCHES

The pin, which once had the very practical purpose of holding clothing together, is the most versatile of jewelry adornments. Attractive as well as fashionable, pins in many kinds of metals and materials enhance a woman's garment at hem, shoulder, pocket, or cuff. Pins can be worn anywhere the wearer wishes—high or low, in back or in front. The pin gives the owner great freedom of choice and, as her most ubiquitous jewel, has few limitations.

There are variations among pins and brooches, and it may be helpful to give some definitions:

Brooch. A brooch is a rigid design mounted on a back that fastens with a pin.

Chatelaine. A chatelaine may consist of two brooches connected by chains or a single large brooch with chains looped below.

Clip. A clip is a brooch design with a pronged, hinged back.

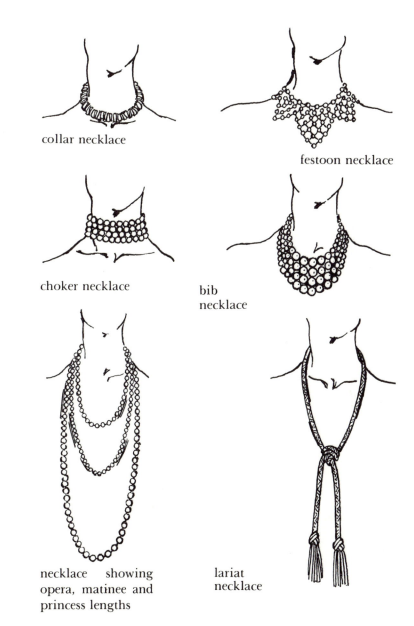

collar necklace

festoon necklace

choker necklace

bib necklace

necklace showing opera, matinee and princess lengths

lariat necklace

convertible necklace

sautoir necklace

pendant necklace

Stickpin. A stickpin is a straight pin with an ornament at the top and a guard protecting the pin.

Pin Pendant. A pin pendant is a brooch equipped with a centered loop so that it can be hung on a chain and used as a necklace as well as a pin.

Many fashionable women, especially entertainers and other personalities, wear favorite pins that in time become established as their personal emblems. Every woman likes to make herself distinctive, and her jewelry, as much as her clothing, can accomplish this for her. To keep pins pleasing to the eye, however, a woman must again remember the simple rules of proportion. Dainty clips and brooches should be worn by smaller women, striking and bold designs by larger women.

Most prized of all is the diamond brooch, which may be combined with rubies, emeralds, and other colored gems. Many designs are original creations of the jeweler and may be abstract or may represent flowers, leaves, birds, fish, dogs, and other animals. Clips, which pinch or grip the material to which the brooch is attached instead of piercing it with a pin, are available in a variety of ornamental and abstract designs displaying a most imaginative use of diamonds and other precious stones.

BRACELETS

From earliest times the bracelet (a name inspired by *bras*, French for "arm") has adorned various parts of the arm. Warriors wore them high on the forearm, above the biceps, to give them extra strength for quicker manipulation of their shields.

Today women wear bracelets to give the illusion of length to hands and fingers. A small, thin wrist looks fuller encircled by a delicate link chain bracelet. A well-rounded wrist appears slimmer in a loose, narrow bracelet. Generally, a discreet number of bracelets on the arm can be graceful, but a woman must not make herself appear to be a jangling mobile.

The main types of bracelets are as follows:

Bangle. A bangle is a stiff, circular bracelet that slips over the hand like a ring. It may be thin (one-fourth inch) or be up to two to three inches in width. It can be plain, textured, polished, round, flat, filigreed, or scroll decorated.

Slave. A slave bracelet is similar to the bangle bracelet but larger and usually worn higher on the arm.

Tab. A tab is a bangle bracelet with one motif or charm hanging from it.

Cuff. A cuff is an oval or round bracelet with a hinge and clasp for greater ease in putting it on the wrist. Because of the hinge, the cuff bracelet fits neatly and stays in place comfortably. Cuff bracelets come in the same decorative themes as bangle bracelets.

Charm. A charm bracelet is a link bracelet with decorative motifs, or charms, hanging from the links. The charms may depict a hobby or other activity, memorable or sentimental occasions, travels, special achievements, children, grandchildren, and so on.

Flexible. A flexible bracelet consists of a number of metal- or stone-set motifs held together with chainlike links and fastened with an invisible or ornate clasp, depending on the design. Flexible bracelets include mesh, stone-set, pearl, and diamond bracelets as well as tailored or stretch hinges.

Spiral. A spiral bracelet is a long length of metal, beads, stones, or pearls that winds around the wrist in a spiral fashion. It may wind around the wrist or arm several times or

charm bracelet

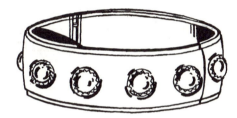

cuff bracelet

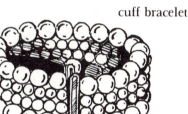

spiral bracelet

flexible bracelet

slide bracelet

Indian or gauntlet bracelet

bangle bracelet

in double or triple width and meet and overlap slightly underneath.

Indian or Gauntlet. An Indian or gauntlet bracelet is a rigid oval bracelet that encircles three-fourths of the wrist with the bottom side open. Such bracelets come in a variety of shapes and may be tapered, wide, flat, richly ornate, highly polished, plain, or gem-studded.

Diamond, Watch, and Pearl Bracelets. The add-a-link diamond bracelet, which is built up a diamond at a time at whatever pace is desired, makes it possible for a woman with a modest budget to include diamonds in her bracelet wardrobe. And the woman who owns two flexible gold or pearl bracelets can clasp them together to make a handsome choker. Bracelet watches, elegant jewelry creations as well as precision timepieces, are most fashionable and add a note of distinction to the well-dressed woman's appearance.

RINGS

The ring, the most popular form of jewelry, draws quick attention to the hand. Quite naturally, small rings belong on small hands and large rings on larger hands; the exaggerated ring is very attractive on long, slender fingers. The woman with small hands, however, does not have to forgo large rings completely. She can wear a dome-shaped ring or one with stones set high.

Rings work magic with jewelers' tricks that give the hand an illusion of tapering slimness. A ring design that leads the eye along the finger rather than across it can lengthen a short hand with broad fingers. Perfect for this effect are marquise-shaped stones and cabochon-cut ovals. To shorten the fingers, a ring design that runs across the fingers will do the trick. The thicker, broader hand appears slimmer with an oval-shaped ring design or an emerald cut or oblong shape. The brilliant cut complements practically every hand—one reason brilliant-cut diamond engagement rings are a traditional favorite.

Fashionable and flattering, rings of many shapes, designs, and colors are worn for dramatic effect on all fingers, often several on a single finger. Rings are set with stones of every kind and hue in countless combinations and are made of gold, silver, and other metals and materials in limitless designs and finishes that range from romantic antique motifs to the bold, modern look.

The following are some of the many types of rings available:

Cocktail Rings. Sometimes called dinner rings, these are massive and are contemporary in design. They usually combine small diamonds and colored stones with gold or platinum.

Friendship Rings. Friendship rings are simple rings given by young people as a pledge of affection and sentiment.

Initial Rings. Initial rings, worn mostly by men, are usually set with flat stones on which one or more initials are applied or encrusted.

Signet Rings. Signet rings generally contain no stones and have monograms, crests, or initials carved into the table of the ring.

Emblematic and Fraternal Rings. Fraternal rings are evidence of membership in military, religious, fraternal, or other organizations and bear the symbol of the organization.

School and Class Rings. School and class rings, worn by many graduates as symbols of their achievement, bear the name of the school or other educational institution, its insignia and the year of graduation.

Eternity Rings. A narrow band of platinum or gold set with a full or half circlet of diamonds and perhaps also colored stones, often given by husband to wife as a pledge of continued love, to mark the birth of a child, or a wedding anniversary. The custom began in England in the 1930's.

WATCHES

Watches, which at first were costly luxuries for royalty and the very rich, have, thanks to technological progress, become one of life's basic necessities. The modern woman, however, has long ceased to regard a watch merely as a handy way to tell time and enable her to keep appointments. Today, a watch can be beautiful.

A contemporary jewelry wardrobe often includes a collection of watches. Depending on a woman's tastes, she can accessorize her fashions with sporty wristwatches, pendant watches, ring watches, whimsical watches worn wherever she likes, traditional pocket watches, and elegantly tailored watches made with precious metals and gems. In short, watches are jewelry as well as timekeeping devices.

COSTUME JEWELRY

Costume jewelry, sometimes called fashion jewelry, is made of a wide assortment of materials. It gives the finishing touch to a woman's ensemble by adding color, form, and eye appeal in exciting fashion designs in keeping with the times.

Costume jewelry is a vital fashion accessory that compels attention and completes a total fashion look.

Costume jewelry is worn by women in all walks of life for fun and fashion. Most costume jewelry is striking, and the best has real beauty. Its designers have to be as much "with it" as fashion experts themselves, and they have proven to be just as original and ingenious with materials. All kinds of metals have been put to use, as well as ceramics, glass, lace, rhinestones, braid, felt, and sequins. Costume jewelry has also been made of wood, leather, and plastics to accessorize bold fashion designs.

Costume jewelry is colorful, original, and provides a ready accent to the changing look of fashion. No matter what the trend in fashion may be, costume jewelry quickly meets it. When high necklines are in, the makers of costume jewelry offer chains, pendants, and other long necklaces. When the shirtdress is popular, costume jewelers keep pace with necklaces that fill in a bare neckline but do not conflict with the garment's collar.

Whatever your personality and taste, do not be afraid to experiment with costume jewelry. The right combination of pieces may express you far better than any single piece by itself. All it takes is some time before the mirror, some imagination and a bit of daring.

Here are some things you should know about better costume jewelry:

1. The design should be original and true to the precise details of the original model.

2. The plating should be of good quality. Thickness, beauty, and fineness in the plating of the metal add to the wear and quality of costume jewelry and give a richer look.

3. The final filing of the metal should give a smooth and beautiful surface. The polishing should be done skillfully so as to bring out and properly situate the glints of the metal.

4. Balance is important. A pin, for example, should be made with such care that it maintains its balance at all times and does not flip down.

5. Clasps on pins and necklaces should be of top quality to insure their safety. They should be so ingeniously hidden as to be unnoticeable.

6. Necklaces should be gracefully constructed to fit and flatter the neck.

7. Stones should be set by hand and perfectly fit. The stones should be of the finest quality and give life and color to the jewelry. Inferior stones are flat and dull.

8. The individual care rendered to each piece of jewelry avoids the mass-produced look of cheap products. Such handwork adds to the quality and the beauty of costume jewelry.

JEWELRY FOR MEN

In recent years men have shown a greater interest in stylish clothing, and jewelry is again proving to be an important accessory to their fashion wardrobe.

The gems most preferred by men include opaque colored stones—the bloodstone, sardonyx, tiger's eye, lapis lazuli, turquoise, jade, carnelian, and malachite. Many men choose cat's-eyes, star sapphires, rubies, moonstones, opals, and aventurine. Among transparent stones, generally the darker-hued ones are popular for men's rings: amethyst, garnet, sapphire, and tourmaline. Men seeking more color and style show a preference for chunky rings with stones of any color that are rough or faceted. Increasing numbers of men choose diamond rings.

The cuff link has always been an index of social rank and distinction. It all started with the button, which was conceived in the thirteenth century by the Saracens. Louis IX of France deserves further recognition in history as the father of the cuff link, for it was he who combined two buttons to form a link and adorned each button with precious or semiprecious stones. By the time Louis XIV reigned, members of the nobility and landed gentry shared with royal families the privilege of wearing cuff links. These linked buttons, of gold and silver, were often set with diamonds, rubies, emeralds, and pearls.

Louis XV was supposed to have acquired an enviable collection of cuff links. Famous for his many amours, the king was fond of matching his bejeweled cuff links to the color of the eyes of his current mistress. Proud of his amatory successes, he also sought to impress lesser ladies of the court. It amused him, so the story goes, to have the royal jeweler summoned to the palace to view the young damsel in current favor and then choose a gem that, set in the appropriate cuff link, would complement her coloring exactly.

Men today can choose from a wide range of cuff link styles to suit every taste—simple and unobtrusive or large and prominent, plain or carved, or perhaps set with stones. Cuff links come in conventional and novel designs with smooth metal surfaces and monograms engraved in distinctive script or motifs that identify a man's interests or hobbies. For evening wear, cuff links are coordinated with studs and are often platinum or white gold set with small diamonds or other precious stones. Cuff links express a man's personality and reflect his individual tastes more than any item of his wardrobe. A famous West Coast attorney (now deceased) is known to have amassed an extensive collection of cuff links during his lifetime, many the gifts of famous and grateful clients in appreciation of his legal talents. He has been quoted as saying that he did not feel fully dressed without his choice of cuff links for the day.

Much of men's jewelry is functional rather than decorative and, in addition to rings and cuff links, includes dress and sports watches that are practical as well as fashionable. A fine watch is a symbol of pride and prestige to the successful man. Other jewelry creations for men include bracelets, pendants, tie tacks and bars, money clips, belt buckles, blazer buttons, studs, cigarette cases and lighters, pillboxes, and such conversation pieces as gold tees, swizzle sticks, or whistles, and silver bar accessories.

Thanks to the enormous upsurge in casual life styles and leisure wear, more and more men are wearing body jewelry—pendants, bracelets, neck chains, odd rings, and even earrings. A few years ago only a few were bold enough to wear these, generally those associated with the arts or the fashion world. Today unisex jewelry is widely accepted and popular.

Neck chains, which began as substitutes for neckties, are made of all metals and designs and often support stones or objects of various kinds—a shark's tooth, a zodiac sign, a gold coin reproduction, a silver chess piece, shells, fossils, and so on—whatever a man chooses to express himself.

BEADS FOR PRAYER AND RELAXATION

In the Middle East, strings of beads, often called "worry beads," are used for counting prayers and for relaxation. The caliphs of Baghdad used beads of rubies and sapphires, and it is still the custom of Muslim peasants to make them from dried olive pits.

Although the real purpose of these beads, called *misbaha* in Arabic, is to count prayers, they have served a variety of uses through the ages. Pre-Islamic witches used them to summon evil spirits, and present-day Coptic priests use them to drive such spirits away. African explorers found them ideal for barter with local tribes, and one Turkish sultan strangled his favorite concubine with her own beads. Arab, Turkish, and

Persian men unconsciously click them through their fingers while contemplating a business deal or even while watching television. An American ambassador in the Middle East carried beads instead of a pack of cigarettes.

No one knows exactly how "worry beads" began. One story is that Cleopatra started the fad by counting and recounting the pearls of a necklace offered by Mark Antony. Four thousand years ago Magi fire worshipers tossed stone beads into the fire during their incantations. Phoenician merchants brought the beads back along with spices from the Far East, and Arab traders used beads to barter for ivory in Central Africa. Wherever the trade routes went, beads proved to be stiff competition for salt as an item of exchange.

Egyptian Copts prescribed a string of ninety-nine beads—one for each attribute of Allah—with a cone-shaped stone at the end. Handier thirty-three-bead strings are popular today, but if the strings are designed for "worrying," they may have any number of beads. Jewish rabbis in Egypt used beads with the Star of David, and the late Imam Ahmad of Yemen prized a set of phosphorescent beads and amazed tribal chiefs by displaying them in a dark room. They glowed, he explained, because they had been touched by the hand of Allah.

While Egyptian Christians take their rosaries to the Coptic Church of Saint Theresa for blessing, Muslims carry their prayer beads to Mecca, where they dip them in the holy well of Zamzam from which the Prophet Mohammed drank during his escape from the desert.

RELIGIOUS JEWELRY

Symbols of faith are worn by many people, probably because of their underlying fear and uncertainty of the present and hope for the future. Religious jewelry, which had waned in popularity some years ago except among Catholics, is once again in demand in many shapes and forms.

The following are some of the more popular items of religious jewelry:

Ankh. This Egyptian hieroglyph in the form of a cross with a loop at the top symbolizes life and is sometimes called the ansate cross.

Chai. The popular Judaic emblem chai used the tenth and eighth letters of the Hebrew alphabet. Combined, they total eighteen, to the Jews the numerical symbol for life.

Cross. The cross, the basic symbol of Christianity, takes many forms: the Latin Cross, with a vertical bar that is longer than the horizontal one, is worn most often; in the Greek Cross, both bars measure the same length; Protestant denominations usually prefer the cross to the crucifix.

Crucifix. A cross with the body of Christ is worn mainly by Catholics and sometimes by Episcopalians and Lutherans.

Flame and Cross. Adopted in 1968 as the symbol of the United Methodist Church, following the union of the Methodists with the Evangelical United Brethren, the flame and cross relate to God the Father by way of God the Son, symbolized by the cross, and God the Holy Spirit, symbolized by the flame.

Mezuzah. A mezuzah is a piece of parchment inscribed on one side with verses from Deuteronomy and placed in a tube as a symbol of Judaism and a reminder of faith in God.

Miraculous Medal. A popular medal for Catholics, the miraculous medal pictures the vision that appeared to Sister Catherine, a member of the Daughters of Charity, in 1830. Graces are promised to those who wear the medal after having it appropriately blessed.

Rose and Heart. The Lutheran rose and heart symbol represents the coat of arms of Martin Luther. The surrounding circle stands for eternity, the stylized rose for the Messianic rose (an old Christian symbol for the coming of the Messiah), and the heart for the love of God.

Sacred Heart Medal. The heart and figure of Christ on the sacred heart medal symbolize devotion to the Sacred Heart among Catholics.

Saints' Medals. Worn by Catholics and sometimes by high church Episcopalians, saints' medals can represent a national, patron, or personal saint.

St. Christopher Medal. St. Christopher is the patron saint of travelers. According to legend, he bore the Christ child across a river. Although St. Christopher is now regarded as a legendary figure, his medal is still in demand among Catholics and Protestants.

Shalom. The traditional Hebraic greeting of hospitality meaning "Peace!" and engraved in Hebrew letters.

Shield. The shield contains a St. Andrew's Cross, used by the Episcopalians, and two rows of five stars, which represent the five wounds of Christ.

Star of David. The star of David is an ancient symbol of Judaism. While its actual origin is unknown, it is possible that the six points of the star denote the days of the week and the hexagon in the center stands for the Sabbath.

SYNTHETIC AND IMITATION STONES

Because natural stones have always been in relatively limited supply and hence rather costly, man has tried again and again to produce them himself. Even the ancient Egyptians sought to simulate the precious emeralds of Cleopatra's mines with green glass. The Romans and Greeks, who also used glass to imitate natural stones, were equally unsuccessful. Such glass reproductions are today known as paste, a term derived from the Italian *pasta* or "dough-like."

It should be noted that the law makes a clear distinction between *synthetic* stones and *imitation* or *simulated* ones. For a stone to be called "synthetic," government regulations require that it possess the same physical, chemical, and optical properties as the genuine stone. Moreover, it must always be identified as a synthetic ruby, sapphire, emerald, or whatever, so as not to mislead the purchaser. An "imitation" or "simulated" stone is just that and must also be identified accordingly.

In the latter part of the nineteenth century, various European scientists sought in vain to reproduce rubies. Since there are many small rubies and few large ones, they finally decided to try melting small stones into big ones. They could not produce the enormous heat needed, however, and their attempts to make rubies in this way met with failure too. Finally the challenge intrigued a brilliant French scientist, Auguste Verneuil, and after many difficulties he invented an oxyhydrogen furnace that was hot enough to melt ruby. He melted down small ruby crystals to create new, larger masses, which he called *boules*, the French word for "balls." The term is still used to describe the synthetic products.

In the beginning these "reconstructed" stones often contained impurities. Later Verneuil used a mixture of pure aluminum powder with chromium oxide added for color and produced synthetic rubies more successfully. Although colorless sapphire and ruby were readily made by this process, blue sapphires required further experimentation and finally were produced by the addition of titanium oxide. After World War

II, Union Carbide scientists, in a search to improve the blue sapphire, accidentally created star sapphires and star rubies.

Unlike rubies and sapphires, emeralds do not melt into a pure liquid and become emerald crystals. To grow emeralds, scientists had to imitate nature by creating the conditions from which emeralds can crystallize from a solution. Many such synthetic emeralds have been developed by scientists for use in jewelry.

Various other synthetic stones have been developed, and, in view of growing demand for precious stones and their steadily dwindling supply, man's ingenuity in the laboratory will probably be responsible for many new ones. Some synthetic stones are beautiful rivals to the genuine ones and can only be distinguished from natural stones by gemological tests.

Imitation and simulated stones of all kinds are widely used in costume jewelry and are often attractive stand-ins for the originals.

JUDGING CRAFTSMANSHIP

When you select jewelry, you should look for indications of quality. Here are some guidelines for judging craftsmanship in jewelry.

Rings. Ring mountings should be sturdy enough for wear. Settings for stones should be smoothly drilled and round, and the underside of the ring shank should be polished to give it a finished look. Prongs should hold stones securely. They should be pushed up close to the stone and should not be jagged. Stones should be set flat, not tipped or tilted.

Brooches. A brooch should be well designed and well proportioned, not clumsy or top-heavy. Stone settings should be round and smooth, with their backs polished and finished.

Safety catches should be substantially made, well soldered to the body, and mechanically perfect.

Necklaces. Holes in necklace beads should be smoothly drilled and accurately centered, and metal links should be firmly closed and of good quality metal so as to withstand wear. Clasps should be relatively easy to open and close, yet have a safety attachment to prevent loss.

Earrings. Both earrings should match in design, be neatly made, well balanced, and comfortable to wear. Earring findings or parts—back, wires, or posts—should be sturdy and in good working order.

Bracelets. Bracelet joints should not rub or interfere with stones. Hinged bracelets should function smoothly, and catches and clasps should be sufficiently well made and strong to hold up under use.

JEWELRY PRODUCTION TECHNIQUES

Here are descriptions of some of the terms that refer to production techniques:

Handwrought. Handwrought jewelry is created entirely by hand, from preparing the metal to making the finished product. It includes melting the metal in a crucible, hammering and bending it to the desired shape, boring and sawing necessary holes by hand, using special tools to engrave textured effects, welding and soldering the parts together, and burnishing and polishing.

Cast. Most fine jewelry pieces are cast in quantity by means of the "lost wax" method. Invented by the ancient Egyptians, the art was lost but rediscovered in 1545 by Benevenuto Cellini, the great Italian goldsmith. Lost again after his death, the "lost wax" process was not rediscovered until the early 1900s by an American dentist, Dr. W H. Taggert, who found it used by a few Italian goldsmiths. It was readily adopted by the dental industry and later in jewelry manufacturing. A model is carefully sculptured in wax and embedded in a special plaster. Before it hardens, the plaster is placed in a vacuum to remove bubbles. Then the wax is burned out—"lost"—and leaves behind a cavity in the form of the original model. The mold is then placed in a centrifugal casting machine that throws molten metal into the cavity. If many castings are desired from one model, the first casting is carefully finished and a flexible rubber mold made from it. Then as many wax replicas as desired are cast in the rubber mold and reproduced in metal like the original. Large molds may be made by fastening many wax replicas together and casting them at one time.

Die Struck. For die struck jewelry, finely machined dies are made to the desired design and shape from a piece of unhardened steel to form a hub. The hub is then hardened and forced into another piece of unhardened steel to make a sunken die. Bar metal is shaped between the two dies by tremendous pressure of a drop hammer. This type of manufacture is used for items that are mass-produced.

Filigree. Filigree is ornamental work in very fine wire featuring flattened, intricate, open designs that often have serrated edges to give a beaded effect.

Damascene. Damascene is the encrustation of background metals with other, usually more precious, metals.

Enamel. Enamel is colored, vitreous glazes, usually fused to the metal base by heat.

Cloisonné. Cloisonné is colored enamel contained within thin strips of metal or wire.

Niello. Niello is a metallic composition of silver, lead, and sulphur having a dull black appearance that is used to fill depressions forming a design.

Engraving. Engraving is inscribing metals with hand-held cutting tools, the oldest means of ornamenting them.

Carving. Carving is similar to engraving except that it involves the removal of more metal or gemstone so that the design is in relief rather than outline.

Milgraining. Milgraining is applying a line of beadlike projections of metal around a setting with a hand tool.

Repoussé. Repoussé refers to beating or punching out sheet metal from the back to produce a raised design.

Embossing. Embossing is creating raised patterns with plates or dies.

Engine Turned. A method of ornamentation by means of a machine or lathe attachment that is capable of producing eccentric relative movement between the rotating mandril and the cutting point so as to form on the work a variety of straight or curved lines.

Tiffany. A tiffany is a setting with six long, slender prongs.

Channel. In a channel setting stones of similar size are placed in a channel to give an unbroken line.

Pavé. Pavé set stones are close together in a flat or domed mounting to show the least possible amount of metal.

Patina. A patina is a thin film on metal. Applying coatings of colored oxides can give metal the effect of aging through natural exposure to the elements. A brushed or burnished surface will give the appearance of age to silver.

CUSTOM-DESIGN JEWELRY

Custom-design jewelry is often the choice of those who cannot find exactly what they want in the jeweler's stock. They may have inherited jewelry that they would like reset in a modern design. Or a man may celebrate the purchase of a yacht or race horse by having a brooch made up in its image as a gift for his wife. A woman may want her engagement and wedding ring to be unique, made for her alone.

These people may or may not be wealthy, but they have in common their own strong preferences. Most jewelers are glad to help translate these ideas into custom-design jewelry and make it up for these special clients.

A rough sketch, not necessarily an artistic one, should be made of the piece of jewelry desired and this submitted with as much information as possible about size, color, shape, and the life-style of the purchaser. Many jewelers can offer helpful suggestions for carrying out the theme. Naturally, the customer must give final approval to the sketch the jeweler makes before he executes the piece.

No one should worry about "breaking up" jewelry that is of sentimental value. A modern design not only enhances the value of the entire piece but takes it out of storage and puts it into use. Jewelry should be worn to be fully appreciated. Thus, resetting and redesigning give new meaning and excitement to precious stones and metals of any age.

ANTIQUE JEWELRY

Many women wear antique jewelry of all kinds and designs, both genuine creations handed down from genera-tion to generation and recent reproductions. Antique jewelry is very appealing to the modern woman of any age who wants to look and feel just a bit old-fashioned in a fast-changing world. Thus dowagers are no longer the only ones who cherish the elaborately crafted pieces of yesteryear.

JEWELRY APPRAISALS

Although most people believe that price evaluation is the most important part of an appraisal, the fact is that an explicit description of the particular item of jewelry is of paramount importance and affords the most protection of all. This description should include the design of the piece, the metal or metals, and the stones.

There are two types of appraisals, each of which is different and cannot serve the purpose of the other. These are:
1. Insurance replacement value.
2. Estate valuation.

Insurance Replacement Value. This type of appraisal is usually needed for the customer to insure his jewelry against loss or damage. The price evaluation in the appraisal should be the approximate cost of replacing the particular jewelry item or recreating it as closely as possible. To accomplish this purpose, the appraisal should take into account current market prices and costs for labor, materials, designs, and stones.

Estate Valuation. This valuation is an appraisal of the cash value of the particular item and is based upon what a willing buyer and a willing seller would agree to without a forced sale. Since it does not consider current market prices or costs for replacement, this type of appraisal is normally lower than that for insurance replacement value.

Your Watch

*E*ver since the dawn of history man has striven to measure time accurately. The sun in the sky was probably his first clock when he realized that its rising and setting divided the day into light and dark periods. He soon discovered that the shadow cast by a stick, stone, or tree changed as the sun traveled across the sky. The lengthening and shortening of the shadow told him not only the general time of the day but also that the seasons were changing.

As man's awareness increased, he developed his first timepiece, the sundial. The sundial goes back to about 2000 B.C.; the Bible refers to it as Isaiah's sundial of Ahaz. The difficulty with this means of telling time, however, was that at best it operated only while the sun was shining. Experimenters tried using water and produced the clepsydra or water clock, derived from the Greek words meaning "to steal water." This device was a container tapered at one end, with a small hole in the bottom. Water was poured into the vessel to a designated mark and allowed to trickle slowly out the hole. The passage of time was measured by the length of time it took for the container to empty itself.

Water clocks were improved, and some were fairly accurate, but their main drawback was that they failed when the water froze or evaporated. Moreover, water clocks could not be used in very dry countries. As a result, a clock was devised that replaced water with sand—the sand clock or hour glass. Sand clocks were originally used by the clergy to regulate the time of their masses and by sailors to gauge the speed of their ships.

The candle clock was still another early timekeeping device. Candles of the same size and material burn at the same steady rate, and by notching them at equal intervals, it was possible to note the number of hours that had elapsed. Oil lamps were also used to measure time; containers were so marked that the passage of time could be inferred from the level to which the oil had burned itself out.

The main disadvantage of all these devices was that they were only partially accurate, measured only short spans of time, and were often a nuisance to keep in operation. From these crude timekeepers, however, evolved the clock and from this the watch.

Early mechanical clocks were driven by mechanical weights and were unreliable. In 1581 Galileo, so the story goes, was in church when he noticed a chandelier swinging over-

sundial

clock

head in a draft. Fascinated by the regularity of its rhythm, he used the beat of his pulse to measure the time intervals of the swings. To his surprise, no matter how far the chandelier swung, it always took the same amount of time to go back and forth. This led to the formation of the principle of the pendulum, a discovery that rendered clocks more reliable. Since pendulum clocks were powered by falling weights, they had to be large and functioned only if kept in a permanent and upright position. The earliest clocks were installed in church towers, town squares, and public buildings. Thus, they could hardly be used as portable timekeeping devices.

About 1500 the invention of the coiled mainspring by Peter Henlein of Nuremberg (which made possible the first portable watch called the "Nuremberg egg") and the development of other new devices by various clockmakers eliminated the need for falling weights and swinging pendulums. One of these new devices was the balance wheel; a hairspring attached to this wheel caused it to swing back and forth.

With a coiled mainspring supplying the power and with the oscillating balance wheel controlling the release of power, a clock could operate in any position and could hence be portable. Of course, no one at that time even dreamed of a small personal clock that could be carried in the pocket or on a chain around the neck. There was, however, a great need for a clock that could be carried by the town watchman, who called out the hours as he made his rounds. The word *watch* originated with these early portable clocks. Since they were used mostly by town watchmen, they were called watchman's clocks. Later they came to be known as watch clocks and finally as watches.

The very earliest watches were made by blacksmiths, who were the skilled mechanics of their day. These watches were so heavy that their owners had to hire page boys to carry them, often suspended by strong chains from their belts. The first watch small enough to fit into a bracelet—the first real wristwatch—made its appearance in 1571 and was proudly presented to Queen Elizabeth I. The early fine watches were usually egg- or ball-shaped, and many had thin cases for pocket wear. One special creation was a watch designed to form the head of a gentleman's walking stick, and craftsmen of the day created many other novelty watches, some with their tiny works set in bracelets, rings, and lockets. The art of watch-making spread to many parts of Europe, particularly Switzerland, still closely identified with the production of fine watches. Mass-production methods, developed from Eli Whitney's idea of interchangeable parts, were first introduced in America in the middle of the nineteenth century and then quickly recognized and accepted by the Swiss. The establishment of time zones in the United States in 1883 increased the importance of conforming to time standards and the demand for accurate timepieces.

Prior to World War I wristwatches were worn mostly by women; men considered them effeminate. When American Army officers wore wristwatches during the war, they became universally popular. Now many innovative wristwatches for both men and women are available—self-winding, water-resistant, shock-resistant, antimagnetic, calendar, electric, electronic, quartz, digital, and so on—in a wide range of styles and prices.

The first mass-produced self-winding watch was made in Switzerland following World War I. Watches have made enormous technological advances over the years. Not only are they precision engineered to insure the utmost accuracy, but in addition many of today's timepieces are beautiful and fashionable pieces of jewelry, often enhanced by precious metals and stones in attractive styles and designs.

Watch cases are gold filled or made of karat gold, rolled gold plate, gold electroplate, stainless steel, silver, platinum, and many other metals and materials.

The most popular watch is the hand-wound watch, which is sturdy and reliable, virtually trouble-free, and adap-

hour glass

stop watch

Three illustrations of time, sundial, inside of clock

table to every conceivable shape and style of case. Essentially, its mechanism consists of a power mainspring and a time-keeping hairspring. As the mainspring unwinds, its power is transmitted through four wheels, called the gear train, to the escape wheel. The pallet fork mediates between the escaping force of the mainspring and the precise hairspring and balance wheel assembly. This two-pronged lever, resembling the flukes of an anchor, is the heart of the mechanical watch and ticks up to ten times per second. While a watch appears to be running continuously, it actually stops and starts up to five times a second. But the parts of a watch are precisely crafted to work together with the least possible friction and vibration. Accuracy is controlled by the balance wheel, which releases the pallet and allows the escape wheel to "escape" one tooth at a time. The speed of the swing of the balance wheel is in turn controlled by the hairspring. All this drives the gears that move the minute and hour hands.

To reduce friction and wear, and to insure greater accuracy and longevity, jewels of synthetic sapphire and ruby are used in watches, especially on the pallet fork. These jewels are far harder than bare metal and can protect strategic points. The importance of the jewels lies in what they do, not in their intrinsic value of only a few cents each. At least seventeen "working" jewels usually protect the points of wear in a good watch.

Automatic or self-winding watches keep themselves wound by the wrist movement of the wearer. An average of two hours' wear should store up enough power to last through at least thirty hours of nonuse. If a person is very active, a slip-clutch mainspring endpiece prevents overtight winding.

Electric watches are powered by small batteries the size of shirt buttons instead of by a mainspring. They do not need winding and will still run if put in a drawer for a long period. Generally, the battery-driven watch is more accurate than a comparable mainspring-driven watch because its power supply is constant. Watch batteries are designed to supply even voltage for almost their entire lives, generally about fifteen months. In electronic watches, transistorized circuits control the flow of electric current.

Another recent development is the watch that has a tuning fork instead of a balance wheel. This fork, actually a miniature version of the musical tuning fork, vibrates between three hundred and four hundred times per second. The quartz-crystal watch is based on the principle that the more rapid the pulse of the frequency standard, the more accurate the time-keeping. In this watch the balance wheel is replaced by a tiny bar of quartz crystal that vibrates thousands of times a second. Because this rate is too high for indexing a mechanical gear train, the vibrations of the quartz are divided down to a much lower frequency, which, in turn, is used to control the display system on the dial. Power is supplied by one or more batteries.

The solid-state watch, or all-electronic watch with no moving parts, is a quartz watch with a digital electronic display instead of a conventional dial with hands. There are two main types—those that light up and those that reflect light. The light-up display is made of light-emitting diodes—hence called LED—for each digit, and from them any number from zero to nine can be formed. Since the diodes light up, they are visible in total darkness. In direct sunlight, however, their luminescence is somewhat dimmed, and some systems have a current booster to increase the brightness in relation to outside light. Because these watches require relatively large amounts of power, they do not have a continuous time display and show the time only when the wearer depresses a button.

The liquid crystal display, known as an LCD, permits the digital display to operate continuously by reflecting available light to make the numbers visible. This system consumes much less power. Solid-state and traditional watches both tell time accurately, but one is a mechanical or electromechanical timekeeper with dial and hands, while the other is a computer with a memory bank that counts and stores information.

Digital watches are often programmed to give more information than the time. They can display the day of the week, date of the month, number of seconds elapsed and some even include calculators and perform additional complex functions. The digital watch of the future may allow one to insert his own particular programming, such as birthdays, telephone numbers, advertising slogans, alarms, time reminders, medical applications and many other individual needs.

Modern watches not only keep accurate time but also serve many unique purposes when equipped with special accessories. Chronograph watches measure small fractions of a second; some buzz an alarm to remind the owner of an appointment; others give the time in various parts of the world. Braille watches for the blind enable the wearer to open the cover and "feel" the time. Special watches are designed for astronauts, pilots, skin divers, doctors, nurses, golfers, walkers, architects, parachutists, engineers, and many others with specialized professions, hobbies, and interests.

Watches tell more than time and often double as jewelry creations in a myriad of designs, shapes, and materials. Many watches are made with precious metals and embellished with diamonds, rubies, sapphires, and other precious stones.

WATCH CARE

Here are hints for proper care of your watch.

—Wind it once a day, preferably in the morning. When you wind it, take it off your wrist so that it can be wound with the thumb and forefinger.

—Although it is hardly possible to overwind a modern

watch, it is best to stop when you feel tension. Underwinding, however, reduces the ability of the mainspring to power the watch for proper accuracy.

—Avoid exposing your watch to sudden extremes of hot and cold.

—Keep your watch away from perfume, powder, loose tobacco, lint, and dust.

—Many watches are water-resistant, which protects them from outside moisture, splashing, or accidental immersion in water. Do not wear a watch while swimming or taking a bath unless you are positive of its degree of water-resistance.

—To ensure its accuracy and long life, your watch should have a checkup at least every two years, especially if it is subject to hard wear or exposure to dust and dirt.

—Use a watch that suits the purpose for which it is worn—dress, business, sports, and so on.

—If your watch has a problem, don't try to fix it yourself. Only an expert watchmaker can put your watch back into working condition and give it the careful attention it deserves.

—Remember that a new watch may need some acclimatization to your wrist. While it may run perfectly when at rest, the type of use you put it to could cause some variation in its functioning. After you have worn it a few weeks, take it back to your jeweler if necessary, and he will make whatever adjustment is needed. Most brand-name watches are guaranteed by the manufacturer for one year against any defects. Many retailers offer their own guarantees for the private brands they sell.

WATCH WORDS

Analog. An analog watch is one where time display is shown in relationship to fixed indicators—e.g., the traditional watch with hands in a relative (or analogous) position to the indicators on the dial.

Antimagnetic. Many people are exposed to weak magnetic fields from television sets, radios, and various appliances; others are exposed to strong magnetic fields from X-ray machines, generators, or transformers that can actually make a watch stop. Watches can be protected from these fields by making parts like the balance wheel and pallet fork of nonferrous metals instead of steel. If a watch becomes magnetized, most watchmakers can remedy the problem in seconds with a demagnetizing machine.

Balance Wheel. The balance wheel is the part of the watch whose vibrations, governed by the hairspring, perform the actual timekeeping indicated by the hands on the dial.

Crystal. About 95 percent of all watch crystals are now made of plastic that is unbreakable, elastic, and inexpensive. Better-quality plastics will also withstand aging, heat, and atmospheric conditions such as humidity. Top-grade thick glass is still used in the crystals of vacuum-case and skin-diver watches. Designers have also used gem materials such as smoky quartz as crystals in fashionable watches.

Escapement. The escapement is the part of the watch that controls the speed of its operation.

Hairspring. The hairspring is the tiny coil of special alloy metal attached to the balance wheel. It maintains the wheel's perfectly spaced oscillations per second.

Mainspring. The mainspring is the power source in a hand-wound or self-winding watch.

Movement. The movement is the mechanical part of the watch. Quality watches have an average of 125 parts, all machined to microscopic tolerances. The two types of movement are the jeweled-lever and pin-lever, named according to whether the prongs of the pallet fork are jewel-tipped or are steel upright pins.

Shock-Resistant. Practically all good watches have a shock-absorbing device at the balance-wheel pivots. However, to qualify as shock-resistant, the watch must be able to withstand a fall from a height of thirty-six inches without damage and without a change in daily rate of over one minute.

Tolerances. The dimensions of a watch are usually stated in hundredths of a millimeter. However, the tolerances—that is, the maximum amount by which parts may vary from specifications—are usually expressed in microns. A micron is about .0007 the thickness of a human hair.

Water-Resistant. A watch may be called water-resistant or water-protected when it meets certain standards of immersion. To meet them, case and crystal must fit snugly, and a seal must accompany a screw-on back. Hand-wound watches should have a well-fitted winding stem complete with high-quality gasket. Under Federal Trade Commission guidelines, a water-resistant watch must not admit moisture after complete immersion in water under atmospheric pressure of fifteen pounds per square inch for at least five minutes, and for another five minutes under a pressure of an additional thirty-five pounds per square inch.

JUDGING A QUALITY WATCH

Here is a summary of how a jeweler judges a quality watch:

1. The case should be well made and of good quality. It should fit as closely as possible to the size and shape of the movement.

2. The dial should be well finished and of uniform color or surface design.

3. The band or strap should be sturdy and well constructed. It should have no rough edges or burrs.

4. The crystal or glass should be polished and clear and of substantial thickness. It should be easy to see the hands.

5. Luminescent material should be applied equally around the dial.

6. The hands, including the second hand, should be straight and rigid. They should be attractive and enhance the appearance of the watch.

7. The crown or winding button should be of proper size and fit. It should be streamlined and close to the case. It should not be too tight and wind easily.

8. A quality watch has a minimum of seventeen working jewels, including the two in the jeweled lever. Watch jewels should be synthetic sapphires which are extremely hard and microscopically shaped and finished. They eliminate friction and guard against wear by avoiding metal-to-metal contact of the parts that do the most work.

The entire watch should show evidence of quality control and high standards of craftsmanship. The best advice is to buy a watch of good name from a reliable jeweler in whom you have trust and confidence.

Four different types of timepieces

Gold: King of Metals

Gold, shining in nuggets in riverbeds, caught the eye of man thousands of years ago. Thus began the romance between man and gold that has persisted through the centuries.

Ever since man first discovered how workable gold was, he has fashioned both beautiful and useful objects from it—prestigious ornaments and jewelry, coins, and sacred religious objects. From the very beginning, man regarded gold as the metal of the gods. Early man's most constant influence was the sun; it warmed him, made his crops grow, and heralded the coming of each new day. Since the color of the precious yellow metal was that of the sun, man used it to worship the sun gods, a tradition found among the Babylonians, Egyptians, and Incas. Monarchs, supposedly semidivine, set the trend for the enjoyment of gold as personal adornment. And, because gold became more and more valuable, it became in time a major medium of exchange.

The Egyptians regarded gold as solidified fire, like the sun, it became the ultimate symbol when they dedicated it to the sun god Ra, whom they revered as the universal creator. The tomb of King Tutankhamen, who died about 1400 B.C., was found to contain a tremendous hoard of gold, as befitted his rank and power. His inner coffin was made of solid gold and weighed forty-four pounds, the largest gold object to have survived from antiquity. A face mask and sandals of gold and most of the gold jewelry Tutankhamen had worn in life—including amulets, anklets, bracelets, rings, crowns, and collars—adorned his mummified body. Even his fingers and toes were tipped with gold.

Obviously, gold was divine to the Egyptians. When Cleopatra visited Caesar, she rode in a barge adorned with vast sheets of gold leaf in many colors. We quote Shakespeare, who wrote that the boat glowed on the water "like a burnish'd throne." Gold was a royal metal to the Greeks, too, and their desire and quest for it is described in their art and literature. The presentation of a gold apple to Aphrodite, goddess of love, started the Trojan War; the hero Jason, with his Argonauts, sailed out intrepidly to bring back the Golden Fleece; King Midas was empowered by the gods to turn everything he touched into gold. Greek temples and statues were adorned with gold, and it became a favorite medium of exchange.

The Bible refers to gold often and speaks of its earthly and spiritual values. King Solomon gave his name to fabled gold mines and used their gold to build a temple in Jerusalem. The New Jerusalem of the New Testament is described as paved with gold.

The "talent," often mentioned in the scriptures as a coin, was actually a weight in the amount of about 8.5 grams; gold served as money and was valued according to its purity and weight. But the constant testing required to make sure the gold was genuine was a time-consuming burden, and for this reason merchants invented coins, each with a definite weight and value of its own. The merchant's seal was often stamped on the coin, and the better his reputation for honesty, the more readily his coins were accepted. The coins of unscrupulous merchants who adulterated them with an inferior metal or misrepresented their weight were less favored.

Merchants usually gave their gold to goldsmiths for safekeeping and received in return paper receipts. These receipts were easier and safer to carry than gold, and when signed by trusted goldsmiths, were as easily negotiable as gold. The goldsmiths, however, mindful of the opportunity to increase their wealth, loaned some of the gold at interest, thus becoming the world's first bankers. Goldsmiths had to be sure that there was enough gold in their vaults to honor the paper receipts for the gold in their custody. In many cities goldsmiths were functioning as bankers and finally the Bank of England was founded by a London goldsmith.

The fall of the Roman Empire temporarily robbed man of all his stored technical knowledge for mining gold. As the supply of gold diminished, his desire to possess it increased even more, and the inventive alchemists of the Middle Ages tried in vain to produce it from other materials. Although their efforts failed, they did succeed in building up a body of knowledge about minerals and other substances that formed the basis for the modern science of chemistry.

In hope of finding a golden Orient, men set sail from Spain. They did not reach the Indies they sought, but the new lands they found in the Western Hemisphere yielded the gold they wanted. As they forced their way through the Caribbean and the Americas, the conquistadores found the gold-rich lands of Mexico and Peru. The Aztecs and Incas fell before them and surrendered gold treasures the Spanish had never dreamed of. Suddenly, once again, Europe was rich in gold and able to transform it into works of art.

Gold is synonymous with warmth and beauty. We speak of golden sunsets, golden harvests, golden leaves, and golden years. A kind person is said to have a "heart of gold," an obedient child is said to be "as good as gold," and our most universal religious tenet is the golden rule.

The scarcity of gold and our universal appreciation of it make it the one constant, worldwide symbol of value. Yet if all the gold ever accumulated in man's history were to be gathered into a single brick, it would fit into the confines of a baseball diamond and weigh but 100,000 tons.

Primitive man found gold by picking up loose nuggets that had been washed and eroded out of rocks deep in the earth. He had no knowledge of mining and must have thought the gold a gift from the gods. Later, although still not fully aware of how to track gold to its sources, men developed a fairly efficient method of gathering even tiny particles from riverbeds. This method, called panning, was used by prospectors and involved considerable labor. When a prospector found a placer mine, which is a deposit of gold-bearing sand or gravel along a stream, he would scoop up a bit of the sand with some water and swirl it about in a circular dish with sloping sides. The water would carry the light sand over the pan's lip and leave the heavier gold at the bottom. Much later, techniques for mining such deposits adapted this method to much larger tray-like containers that sometimes spanned the whole stream. Amateur prospectors still engage in gold panning in certain parts of this country and have even developed their own championship contests.

The Egyptians discovered an efficient method for extracting ore from the rock in which it was contained. They would drive shafts into quartz veins in the earth, light a fire against the rock face and wet the hot surface with cold water, then crack the rock and break it loose. The ore was freed, then broken, crushed, milled, and spread over a slanting table. The workers poured water over this and washed away the sand and crushed rock to leave a gold-bearing deposit on the board. The final steps were like a refined method of panning, but the entire process was the first mining of gold from its ore.

Even these methods were largely lost during the Middle Ages, and no major advances were made until the famed gold rushes of the nineteenth century in California, the Yukon, and Australia, which attracted adventurers from all over the world and led to many innovations in gold mining.

Major deposits of gold were discovered in South Africa, where now the most modern techniques are used. Shafts are sunk deep into the earth, and horizontal underground tunnels link and connect in a complex system. Underground pump stations and workshops, power lines, compressed-air columns, reservoirs, ventilation fans, telephone systems, and other devices are standard equipment in gold mining today.

Fashioning gold into ornamental objects is an ancient art. Neolithic diggings in Ireland and France abound in gold, and gold beads have been found among the remaining bones of these prehistoric peoples. The ancient Sumerians, Babylonians, and Assyrians apparently prized gold bracelets, rings, urns, chalices, and statues, and many museums are especially proud of their displays of Egyptian jewelry unearthed by archeological excavations. The jewelry of the early Egyptians combined gold with such gems as amethysts, carnelian, lapis lazuli, and turquoise. The Egyptians also developed great skill in the use of enamel with gold.

Ancient Greek and Mycenaean jewelry took the form of thin gold discs that were sewn onto clothing. The designs—usually butterflies, grasshoppers, and forms of sea life—were first carved on wooden discs, then covered with a thin sheet of gold that was hammered into the grooves of the woodcut.

Probably the finest goldsmiths prior to the Renaissance were the Etruscans, who were known as a gold-wearing people. Their jewelry was extremely fine. One of the most interesting features of Etruscan jewelry was the granulation of surfaces, a method of working gold that made more economical use of their limited supplies of gold. By means of this process—which involved the adherence of tiny, hollow gold spheres to a thin gold-sheet backing with no signs of soldering—these skilled goldsmiths achieved the look of a large quantity of gold. This method was lost for centuries until the great goldsmiths of the Renaissance rediscovered it. Color in the old Etruscan work was supplied by cloisonné enamel or by dark blue pastes.

The outstanding quality of gold is its capacity to last forever. Gold does not rust like iron nor tarnish like copper or silver, for it is chemically inactive and cannot be corroded by air, water, or common acids. It has been buried by one civilization after another and dug up again and again, and always it emerged in perfect condition. Despite the softness of the metal (which makes it so easily workable), an article of gold can be depended on to keep its beauty for future generations.

One ounce of gold can be drawn into a wire more than fifty miles long, and a small bit of it can be hammered into gold leaf so thin that as many as 250,000 leaves would make a pile only one inch high.

Renaissance means "rebirth," and the period certainly was that. The old techniques of classical times were once again taken up, and new ideas and methods were invented by the artists who worked in gold. The creations of the sixteenth-century master goldsmith, Benvenuto Cellini, influences fine gold work today, even as his designs were often inspired by the ancient craftsmen. Famous masters in art, Leonardo da Vinci and Michelangelo among them, began their training as apprentice goldsmiths. This tradition for high artistic standards has profoundly affected the design of jewelry to the present day.

The greatest use of gold in the United States is for jewelry, and modern methods of production make gold jewelry today even more beautiful than that of the past. Gold can be alloyed with other metals for use in jewelry that is intended to receive considerable wear. This makes it harder and can alter its color if desired. The addition of silver to gold makes it paler; copper makes it reddish; cadmium and silver, greenish; iron, bluish; and nickel or palladium, white. A goldsmith can test whether a metal is actually gold by rubbing some off on his touchstone and adding a drop of nitric acid. Whatever is not gold will bubble away. This is the origin of the expression "the acid test."

Fine gold, which is 99.9 percent pure, is called 24-karat gold, but it is too soft for making jewelry. The most popular gold used today is 14- or 18-karat gold. In the case of 14-karat gold, the alloy contains 14 parts gold by weight and 10 parts another metal or metals; 18-karat gold consists of 18 parts gold and 6 parts other metals. Somewhere on the piece of jewelry is stamped the manufacturer's trademark and an abbreviation denoting the quality of the gold. In the United States no item containing less than 10 karats of gold may be sold as gold.

The origin of the 24-karat standard for pure gold dates back to Roman goldsmiths who tested gold for authenticity. They, too, used the smooth, black stone known as a touchstone. The mark made on the stone by rubbing it with the golden object under scrutiny was compared with marks made by the goldsmith's twenty-four touch needles suspended from wire rings. Three sets were used—one set made of varying proportions of gold and silver alloy, another of gold and copper, and a third combining all three metals. The first needle on the ring contained only one part of gold to twenty-three parts of the metal with which it was alloyed. The proportion of gold in each needle increased up to the twenty-fourth, which was pure gold. Hence, 24-karat gold became the accepted standard of pure gold, and from this process was derived the division of gold into that many parts.

The choice of many different alloys, each with its own characteristics, allows modern jewelry designers to combine gold in the most attractive way with gems—an impetus to the art that was undreamed of by early craftsmen. Another innovation in gold jewelry is the wide range of exciting finishes and textures, developed through improved technology, that make gold jewelry even more attractive; in addition to the mirror bright finish, gold can be worked with florentine, brush, matte, and polished finishes that bring out the warm glow of the metal. With the use of textures—including moss, bark, bamboo, mink, and diamond—it is possible to create the look of bulk combined with lightness that ancient goldsmiths sought to achieve.

In India a bride's social status as well as her financial security are determined by the amount of gold jewelry she receives at her wedding. Since women are generally not allowed to own property, this gold jewelry is her life insurance policy and credit card combined.

It is still believed by many that gold can kill infections and prolong life. A Japanese hotel features the biggest golden bathtub in the world, weighing over three hundred pounds. A dip in the tub, it is claimed, adds a year to one's life.

Americans can now legally own or deal in gold bullion, gold dust, gold nuggets, and gold coins. The coins are used in many kinds of jewelry—pendants, earrings, rings, charms, cuff links, belt buckles, money clips, tie tacks, studs, blazer buttons, and so on—and have become increasingly popular.

Many objects can be made of gold, and the inventive jewelry manufacturers produce an endless variety—gold keys, whistles, pillboxes, identification bracelets, money clips, golf tees, toothpicks, bookmarks, telephone dialers, key chains, wallet covers, collar stays, garters, hairpins, safety pins, spoons, lighters, and many other novelties.

Gold jewelry flatters women of all ages and can be worn at all times of day, with stones or without. A wardrobe of gold jewelry includes pins, bracelets, earrings, clips, necklaces, pendants, watches, and rings of all kinds. In rings the most traditional use of gold is the wedding band, but there is such a choice of fashionable and novelty rings today that the ring-loving Romans would be envious.

Because of its value, gold has been often imitated. In the eighteenth century an enterprising goldsmith in England named Christopher Pinchbeck made a gold-looking alloy of copper and zinc that he fashioned into fake jewelry. He sprinkled his creations with gems of glass and paste and sold them to servant girls who wanted to look like ladies and to ladies who were afraid of thieves.

The development of gold-filled jewelry, which is made by mechanically bonding a layer of karat gold to a reinforcing metal, is the result of an accidental discovery made by a Sheffield silversmith named Thomas Bolsover in 1740. Bolsover was mending a crack in a sterling knife when he found that his vise was not tight enough. He wedged in a copper coin, and while applying heat to the knife, he was suddenly distracted by the town crier's announcement of some urgent news. When he returned his attention to the knife a few moments later, he saw

that it was fused to the copper coin. The blade was ruined, but the process that came to be known as the "Old Sheffield" was born. Bolsover realized that he had found a way to fashion products out of precious metals, and his method was later adapted to gold. Since gold-filled jewelry uses less gold than karat-gold articles, it is naturally lower-priced and is available to many more people.

According to government standards, gold-filled jewelry must have a layer of at least 10-karat gold that weighs at least one-twentieth of the total weight of the metal. If this layer is 14-karat gold, for example, and is one-tenth of the total weight, it should be marked "1/10 14K Gold Filled" or "1/10 14K G.F."

An article with less gold than required for gold filled is called gold plated or rolled gold plated. In such cases the fraction indicating the weight ratio must precede the quality mark and the article should bear, for example, the designation "1/40 14K G.P." Gold plate and rolled gold plate are abbreviated as G.P. and R.G.P., respectively. In recent years new methods of electroplating have prompted the Federal Trade Commission to rule that any jewelry coated with at least seven-millionths of an inch of gold can be called gold electroplate, and that coatings of one-hundred-millionths of an inch can be called heavy gold electroplate. Terms such as "gold washed" and "gold flashed" may be applied to an electrolytic finish less than seven-millionths of an inch thick.

To protect the public, the National Stamping Act requires that all quality marks for gold and silver must be accompanied by the registered trademark or trade name of the manufacturer or seller. The purpose of this law is to make it possible to identify the maker of an improperly marked item of gold or silver. Criminal sanctions and civil remedies are provided to enforce the intent of this law.

Calima gold "ring like"
figure

Gold winged figure
with long tail

Quibmaya gold alli-
gator

Calima gold statue

Calima U-shape design
with tiny gold rods

Gold face mask with
eyes cut out

126

Silver: Queen of Metals

*I*n very ancient times silver was even more precious than gold because it was harder to find. The burial mounds of primitive man offer proof that he used silver. Silver diadems of prehistoric origin have been found in Spain, and silver ornaments have been unearthed from Chaldean tombs dating as far back as 4500 B.C.

The first silver jewelry was worn by women about their necks and consisted of pebble-shaped pieces of silver that later evolved into chains and finally filigree. Such ornaments are still popular in certain parts of the world, as are adaptations of these necklaces that are worn in the form of silver rings suspended from the ears. Some Egyptian women wear silver anklets, called *halalils*, and in India silver anklets are matched by bracelets. Long ago, silver collars were fashionable attire for the women of Spain, and silver was part of the Chinese bride's apparel. In Tibet silver ornaments made in various designs and religious symbols adorned women's headdresses. Tibetan women also wore silver earrings, pins, brooches, clasps, charms, bracelets, and rings and even used silver in their embroidery.

The Greeks had a great love for silver and associated it with the goddess Diana, and Homer refers to awards of silver vessels and silver wine cups. The Greeks made and wore silver jewelry of all kinds, and some of their heroes even had shields of silver.

Silver is mentioned many times in the Bible. It was part of Abraham's wealth and was used to buy the burial plot for his wife, Sarah. The ancient Jews were excellent silversmiths and created many beautiful objects of silver. When Joseph gave his brothers a sack of grain in answer to their plea, he commanded that it contain "my cup, the silver cup" as a gesture of friendship.

In addition to its beauty and usefulness, silver has had considerable religious significance. Because of its color, man has associated it with the moon; the ancient Chinese called the moon the "silver candle" and the Milky Way the "silver river." The Egyptian god Ra was supposed to have bones of silver, and in Hindu mythology one of the three fortresses of heaven was silver. To this day married Hindu women wear silver bangles and toe rings. Muslims believe that the second heaven is made of silver, and many Muslim charms are written or mounted in silver to increase their effectiveness. The traditional act of formalizing the death of a pope is touching his forehead three times with a silver hammer and calling out his baptismal name; and at the coronation of a British monarch, fifteen silver trumpets are sounded.

Silver has also been associated with magic. A Persian legend tells of a silver statue that always laughs at hearing a lie. An old superstition is that a silver bullet will kill a ghost, sorcerer, witch, giant, or anyone who leads a charmed life. Count Dracula, as a vampire, could be killed only with a silver bullet or a stake through his heart. In the Middle Ages silver nails were often used to make a coffin or to secure the lid, to make sure the spirit of the departed would not escape. Even today, silver charms and countercharms are used all over the world. In China a silver locket around a child's neck is believed to protect him from evil spirits. In parts of France couples on their way to be married encircle themselves with a silver chain so they will not be bewitched en route. American Indians are known for silver jewelry of all kinds, and the Navahos ritually wore little silver bells in their tribal dances. A gypsy's hands are supposed to be crossed with silver so that she can better predict the future.

Silver is the whitest of metals and the most lustrous. It has the greatest reflectivity and is an excellent conductor of heat; it is pleasant to touch and taste and so is a favorite for tableware. Silver is one of the easiest metals to work with because it is so versatile. It can be cast, stamped, burned, hammered, chased, engraved, pierced, wired, filigreed, damascened, inlayed, electroplated, and embroidered. It can be drawn into wires finer than human hair and hammered into sheets so thin it would take 100,000 of them to make a stack an inch high.

Silver is harder than gold but softer than copper. Because it is too soft in its pure state to be practical for commercial use, silver is usually mixed with copper to form an alloy. Through the ages the percentage of pure silver in solid silver has varied greatly. Not until the year 1300, by decree of Edward I of England, was a definite standard established. "No manner of vessel or server shall depart out of the maker's hands," ruled Edward, "until it can be assayed by the warden of the craft, and further that it be stamped with a leopard's head." This standard, 925 parts of pure silver to 75 parts of copper, is known as sterling and was adopted in the United States in 1906 as part of the National Stamping Act.

The word *sterling* may have been derived from a group of German traders, the Easterlings, who came to England often in the seventeenth century to buy various goods. They always paid for their purchases with pieces of bright silver of uniform purity and in time these were called Easterlings, too. When the British adopted the high standard of 92.5 percent fine as a quality ratio for silver, the name evolved into *sterling*.

Silver has a long history in Germany, too. It was produced in a town in Bohemia called Joachimsthal, and originally the silver coins minted there were known as *Joachimsthalers*. They later became *thalers* and finally *dollars*.

Until the Middle Ages silver was a luxury reserved for royalty and the very rich. Few households could afford table utensils of silver, and distinguished guests often brought their own folding sets with them. The flowering of the arts in the Renaissance saw the emergence of silversmithing in the monasteries and as an art practiced by Cellini and by others in France and England. Many of the most beautiful creations of these early silversmiths were designed for use in churches: chalices enriched with gems and enamels, crosiers, crucifixes, altar fronts, and similar religious objects.

In England silversmiths formed a guild in 1180 and initiated the custom of branding silverware with the mark of the maker. Of all the articles made of silver, none surpassed the silver bed Charles II ordered for his mistress Nell Gwyn in

1674, one of his numerous lavish silver gifts to her. Others included tables, stands, andirons, sconces, vases, and clocks. To please this silver-loving monarch, the city of London presented him with a silver table weighing eight thousand ounces. The table was added to his royal collection but has somehow been lost. During Queen Anne's reign, silver toys for children were very popular, and silversmiths created tea sets, dollhouses, furniture, carriages, soldiers, animals, and other miniatures to amuse the young.

Silversmithing was an art in the New World long before Columbus landed on its shores. Aztecs in Mexico and Incas in Peru used silver for objects of all kinds as well as for jewelry. When Cortés came to Mexico in 1519, silver wares were being sold in the streets of many Aztec towns and villages, but when he first saw the silver mines at Taxco, he presumed the metal was tin and mined it to make guns.

The first silver made by the American colonists was simple and useful, for silversmiths were among the earliest settlers. The passenger list of one early ship bound for Virginia in 1608 included "two goldsmiths, two refiners and a jeweler," and before long New England became the center of the industry. Robert Sanderson arrived in Boston from London and formed a partnership with John Hull, and their work and that of their contemporaries is admired to this day for the simplicity of its lines and the grace of its forms.

Sanderson and Hull made the first known American pieces, including beakers, chalicelike cups for churches, tankards, caudle cups, and porringers. Hull minted the first silver coin in America, the famous Pine Tree shilling, which was actually illegal because the British had forbidden the colonists to mint their own money.

The most renowned of all American silversmiths was Bostonian Paul Revere, whose historic midnight ride apparently outranked any of his other achievements. His father,

Appolos de Rivoire, who had come to the colonies from France, was apprentice to John Cooney. He had changed his name to Paul Revere, then in 1723 went into business for himself. He was so successful as a silversmith that he was well able to support a wife and twelve children. Upon his death his son Paul took over the enterprise and in time became an expert silversmith and a skilled engraver as well. Few craftsmen could finish a complete piece of silver down to and including the engraving as he did. We have already mentioned his Revere bowl, a silver classic that is still widely popular.

As a matter of fact, Revere's talent as an engraver led him into politics when he began to do political cartoons poking fun at the British. Revere, a versatile man, was also a powder manufacturer, a jeweler, an ironmaster, a brazier, and a printer. He was also a proficient dental craftsman, and his advertisement in a Boston newspaper in 1768 proclaimed his ability to make artificial teeth from gold and silver wire to replace natural ones.

By about 1800 the art of silversmithing was thriving, but soon the advent of machines led to its decline. Bolsover's accidental discovery of Sheffield plate in 1740 in England had made it possible to fuse plates of copper and silver together with heat. Now a bar of copper covered with a sheet of silver could be rolled out and made into hollowware. Thus, Sheffield was our first inexpensive silverware.

Another practical development was a metal called Britannia, which was made of tin, antimony, and copper and contained no silver. This alloy was almost as brilliant as silver, which it resembled, and was widely used in many kinds of hollowware. It was sometimes plated with silver.

In the early nineteenth century a way was found to plate copper by means of electricity. This electroplating process was a far simpler method than the old Sheffield one. In modern silverplating blanks of metal to be plated are dipped into vats of a silver cyanide solution. Blanks are the first rough outlines of the items. The blanks are placed at the negative pole of a battery, and bars of pure silver at the positive pole. The current is turned on and the molecules of silver flow with the electricity from the positive to the negative pole, thus plating the blanks. The thickness of the plating is determined by the strength of the current and the length of time it is used. An extra plate of silver is often applied on the areas of greatest wear. The silver used is "925 fine," which means that it contains 925 parts of pure silver to 75 parts of copper (for added strength).

In the nineteenth century some silverware was marked "coin silver" because it was made of 900 parts silver to 100 parts copper, the same proportions used by the United States Government to mint its coinage. Since 1966, dimes, nickels, quarters, and half dollars have consisted of a wafer of copper sandwiched between layers of copper-nickel alloy.

SILVER JEWELRY

In the days before platinum and white gold were used for making fine jewelry, silver was often used. When set with precious stones, silver required highly skilled craftsmanship. Because silver is more abundant than other precious metals and not so costly, it was not surprising that it became very popular and fashionable in jewelry. Recent interest in American Indian jewelry has stimulated a renewed demand for silver. Much of today's silver jewelry is coated with rhodium or a lacquer finish to prevent tarnishing.

Liquid silver—long, thin metal tubes cut about one-eighth of an inch in diameter and one-half inch long and strung like beads—has attracted considerable fashion interest and is often combined with various stones in necklaces, pendants, bracelets, and earrings.

Either gleaming or antiqued, silver jewelry shows many unique qualities. Stones set off its shine in pendants and bracelets, and sculptured silver is beautiful when worn high on the throat. Spoon rings, often reproducing a favored silver pattern, are very popular. Modern designs lend themselves to the sheen that silver gives to rings, earrings, pins, and pendants, and the use of yellow gold with silver creates a striking effect.

PEWTER

Modern pewter is almost entirely made of tin, with a small proportion of other metals added to harden and strengthen it.

Like tin, pewter has a very long history. As with gold, silver, and platinum, the value of a pewterware item depends not only on its esthetic beauty and craftsmanship but also on the actual weight of the metal itself. Heavier and more expensive items are usually produced by a casting process and lighter ones by modern manufacturing methods such as spinning or stamping.

From early times, pewterers, like goldsmiths and silversmiths, have banded together into craft guilds to protect their standards of materials and workmanship. The most ancient piece of pewter known is the tin "pilgrim bottle" of Abydos, in Egypt, dating back to about 1500 B.C. Pewter was used in Roman times, as indicated by Pliny, who wrote in the first century A.D. that a tin vessel improved the taste of wine.

Pewter lends itself readily to simple casting in clay or metal molds and was thus an ideal early candidate for use in drinking vessels. From the utilitarian beakers and cups of

earlier times, pewter items have evolved into tankards and gob-
lets of all kinds, because the metal is pleasing to the touch, elegant in appearance, and makes drinking more pleasurable.

Pewter has gained great popularity in modern jewelry
because it has many natural advantages. It is soft enough to be
readily worked; it does not harden when deformed; and it is
readily soldered. Moreover, it combines well with gems and
can be electroplated. Pendants, rings, bracelets, and brooches
can be created in many styles and designs, and their attractiveness can be enhanced by coloring, engraving, and etching.

Platinum: The Noblest Metal

*I*n the early part of the eighteenth century the natives of Colombia in South America wore ornaments made from a bright metal that Europeans had never seen before. Originally, it was considered to be a waste product of little value from gold-mining operations, and it was a long time before it was recognized as a precious metal. When the Spaniards came to South America to mine gold, they often found it mixed with a silvery-looking metal they regarded as a nuisance because it was so difficult to separate from the gold they sought. They called it *platina*, meaning "little silver," and this is how platinum got its name.

Later platinum came to the attention of European scientists, who realized that it was a new substance to them and one that had many valuable qualities. They discovered, too, that it was actually one of a family of metals. Platinum is the most important of these; the others are palladium, rhodium, iridium, osmium, and ruthenium.

By the 1920s "little silver" had achieved such importance that nearly two-thirds of the platinum mined was used in the United States. When the Koh-i-noor diamond was set into a new English crown in 1937, the metal chosen was platinum because it would hold the gem safely and yet reflect its beauty. Platinum is a soft but tough metal and is generally alloyed with iridium, its sister metal, to provide maximum strength and beauty.

Because of the unique qualities of platinum, it has been in such increasing demand by modern industry that its cost has risen enormously. Its uses range from application in cardiac pacemakers to its function as the catalyst in catalytic converters, which reduce pollutants in automobile exhaust. Platinum is extremely durable and cannot be corroded by potent acids; it never rusts or tarnishes. Jewelers often use white gold or palladium alloy as substitutes for platinum. In many diamond rings the prongs are made of platinum and the remainder of karat gold. Settings of platinum are used for expensive diamond jewelry where the cost of the metal is a relatively minor factor.

Palladium, which is about half as heavy as platinum and costs about a third as much, is an important member of the platinum group. Its lightness is a ready means of distinguishing it from platinum, and jewelry craftsmen often use palladium to eliminate excess weight from earrings, brooches, and the like. Many diamond setters prefer palladium because of its working properties. "Jewelry palladium," an alloy of palladium hardened with ruthenium, is generally used for making jewelry.

Rhodium, another member of the family and the most reflective of them all, is harder and whiter than even platinum and is widely used for plating. Silver, white gold, and platinum are often rhodium plated.

Iridium and ruthenium are effective in alloying platinum for jewelry-making. Osmium, the hardest of all metals, is the most difficult to work and is rarely used by jewelers.

Platinum metals are recovered from the beds of certain rivers of Russia, Colombia, and Alaska and from ores mined in South Africa and Canada. Other countries produce but small amounts. In all these deposits, platinum occurs together with other platinum metals. Seldom is one platinum metal found without some of the others.

Answers to Often Asked Questions

ost of us, when considering the purchase of a gem, jewel, or other precious jewelry item, are apt to ask the jeweler for help. The professional jeweler is, of course, your best authority on everything about jewelry, from romantic lore to up-to-date technical information.

According to a survey by the Jewelry Industry Council, the following are the questions most often asked of jewelers by the public.

1. What makes a diamond so costly?

First, diamonds are exceedingly rare. Even in the diamond-bearing earth of South Africa, only about one part in 21 million is diamond. To find a rough diamond that can be cut and polished into a one-carat gem, workers must blast, dig, crush, and sort over 250 tons of ore. Second, in the process of skillful cutting, a diamond is likely to lose more than half its weight. The value of a diamond depends on four factors—the jeweler calls them the four *C's*—color, cut, clarity, and carat weight. These factors must be considered together to determine the price.

2. How can I best care for my jewelry?

Most jewelry is strong and durable and needs no special care or maintenance, but you can add to its life and beauty by following these simple suggestions:

Diamonds. Diamonds are the hardest of all gems, but even they need a little care to keep them looking their best. Keep them neatly separated in a lined jewel box; if jumbled together, one diamond can scratch another. Have your jeweler check the settings at least once a year to be sure that they are secure and the diamonds are in no danger of falling out accidentally. Protect diamonds from harsh liquids and from being struck sharply on their edges. Have your jeweler give them a professional cleaning periodically. Between such cleanings, soak them occasionally in warm, soapy water, rub them gently with a small, soft brush—an old toothbrush will do nicely—rinse in a solution of a few drops of clear ammonia and warm water, and then dry them on a soft towel.

Emeralds, Sapphires, Rubies, and Other Transparent Gems. Keep other transparent gems separate from each other and from diamonds. The harder gems will scratch the softer ones. All these gems should be protected from sharp blows, harsh liquids, and dust. Have your jeweler check their settings and clean them occasionally, They may be cleaned like diamonds.

Pearls. Pearls are one of the few organic gems and need special care. They should be kept in jewel boxes when not being worn. After each wearing, wipe off body acids with a soft chamois and protect them from perfume, perspiration, water, and other liquids. If needed, give them a quick dip in a mild soap solution and rinse. Have your pearls restrung by your jeweler at least once a year, more often if worn frequently.

Turquoise. Turquoise should be protected from soap, grease, or other substances that might discolor it. Since turquoise fractures comparatively easily, it should be treated with care.

Opals. Like turquoise, these gems should receive tender, loving care. They should be handled and stored carefully and be especially protected from intense heat.

Watches. Watches should be taken to the jeweler for cleaning and adjustments. For other hints on watch care, see Chapter 10.

Silver. Use a good silver polish and rub the piece briskly. Wash it thoroughly in hot, soapy water, and rinse in clear, hot water. Dry with a soft cloth.

Gold. Gold jewelry that is not set with stones may be soaked in a warm, soapy solution to loosen coatings of make-up, cream, and soap. Follow with a quick rinsing in clear, warm water and a final, gentle rubbing with a jeweler's polishing cloth. Or use a good professional dip recommended or sold by your jeweler.

Costume Jewelry. Costume jewelry should be treated gently, because glued stones can become unset in warm water. These pieces should be wiped often with a soft, damp cloth. This is also the best way to keep imitation or simulated pearls clean.

3. *What is the most up-to-date wedding anniversary list?*

Because weddings are so highly regarded, it follows that wedding anniversaries are celebrated with meaningful gifts. Over the years various lists of wedding-anniversary gifts have evolved, no two of which are identical. Many older lists marked the early milestones of marriage with paper, cotton, tin, and such. While anniversary sentiments may not have changed with modern times, there is little doubt that taste in gifts have.

To mark wedding anniversaries with memorable yet functional gifts, the Jewelry Industry Council developed a "Modern Wedding Anniversary List." It has been widely adopted by the general public and appears in leading reference books, almanacs, diaries, and other publications. This list combines traditional gift suggestions with modern practical ones that conform to the changing cycles of American family life.

The first nine anniversaries concentrate on gifts for the home. These are the formative years during which the husband and wife are furnishing their home and accumulating accessories.

The tenth through fifteenth anniversaries are years when the children usually are sufficiently grown up to enable the parents to go out more often, and the gifts suggested are expressions of love.

The cycle returns again to the home for the next four years, the sixteenth through the nineteenth, when the children are old enough to have pride in their home and want to entertain friends.

After a score of married years, the gift list turns to gems and jewelry for personal adornment.

Modern Wedding Anniversary List

1. Clocks
2. China
3. Crystal and glass
4. Electrical appliances
5. Silverware
6. Wood
7. Desk sets—pen and pencil sets
8. Linens and laces

9. Leather

10. Diamond jewelry

11. Fashion jewelry and accessories

12. Pearls or colored gems

13. Textiles and furs

14. Gold jewelry

15. Watches

16. Silver hollowware

17. Furniture

18. Porcelain

19. Bronze

20. Platinum

25. Silver Jubilee

30. Diamond

35. Jade

40. Ruby

45. Sapphire

50. Golden Jubilee

55. Emerald

60. Diamond Jubilee

4. Why does my gold ring cause a smudge on my finger?

While gold does not normally tarnish or corrode, chemical reactions occasionally occur due to various circumstances. One possibility is that an individual's skin secretions may combine with gold or copper molecules in a gold alloy and form dark-hued salts. This sometimes happens to a woman who is pregnant as the result of changes in her body chemistry.

Outside influences may be to blame as well, such as maritime or semitropical climates where chlorides from the sea combine with normal skin secretions to form corrosive chemicals. A person may work in a plant where sulfides and skin secretions will tarnish a ring, or corrosion can be the result of chemicals in cosmetics and detergents.

A change to white gold or gold of a higher karat fineness often solves the problem. In rare instances, one may have an actual allergy to gold or to other metals in the alloy. A simple solution is to have the ring plated with pure gold or another metal such as rhodium.

5. If diamonds are so hard, why did my diamond chip?

While the diamond is the hardest material in the world, it may be chipped or broken if given a sharp blow against a hard object. Remember, a diamond has a direction or cleavage plane along which it can be split, like a piece of wood. While accidental damage of this kind is exceedingly rare, one must be careful to avoid the possibility.

6. If it looks like a diamond and can cut glass, is it a real diamond?

Glass can be scratched by many materials, among them zircons, spinels, sapphires, and rock crystals. The safest way to ascertain whether a stone is a diamond is to check with an expert. To be a diamond a stone must have certain gemological characteristics possessed by no other gem.

7. How do I know I'll get my diamond back from repair or remounting?

The vast majority of jewelers are scrupulously honest and value your faith and confidence more than anything else. If you harbor any doubts about your jeweler, seek a reliable jeweler with an established reputation in your community.

8. What is the most important quality in colored stones?

Color. The pigeon blood of the ruby, the rich green of the emerald, and the cornflower blue of the sapphire are examples of ideal colors especially prized in colored stones.

9. What is the Mohs' scale?

Mohs' scale is the most commonly used scale of relative hardness of minerals and runs as follows: diamond, 10; corundum (e.g., ruby and sapphire) 9; topaz, 8; quartz, 7; feldspar, 6; apatite, 5; fluorite, 4; calcite, 3; gypsum, 2; talc, 1.

The divisions in this scale are not equal, having been chosen arbitrarily by the German mineralogist Friedrich Mohs (1772-1839). The difference between 9 and 8 is considerably greater than between any of the lower numbers, and the difference between any of the lower numbers, and the difference between 10 and 9 is even greater than between 9 and 1. The

Mohs' scale is strictly a relative one in which any mineral higher on the scale scratches those that are lower. In actual hardness, for example, the diamond has been found to be up to 150 times as hard as corundum, the next lower on this scale.

10. What are the most expensive gems?

The largest diamonds are the most costly stones, but large-size rubies and emeralds of fine quality and color are so rare that they may cost even more per carat than diamonds of comparable weight.

11. Are gems a good investment?

Gems are bought primarily for their unique beauty and as an expression of sentiment rather than as an investment. While gems often appreciate in value over the years, this is not the primary reason for owning them.

12. Should I have my jewelry appraised?

It is prudent to have one's jewelry appraised for insurance and inheritance purposes by a competent appraiser.

13. Can you tell a pearl is genuine by biting it?

A natural or cultured pearl (unlike an imitation or simulated one) rubbed against the edge of one's tooth produces vibrations one can actually hear.

14. What is the definition of antique jewelry?

In the United States an article to be imported as an antique must have been made prior to 1830. The widespread popularity of antique jewelry designs has stimulated the manufacture of reproductions of antiques of many kinds.

15. Why should a watch be cleaned periodically?

Periodic cleaning removes dried, gummed-up oil that can increase the friction and wear on the moving parts of the watch and affect its efficiency and accuracy.

16. Can the color of a diamond be changed?

A development in diamond technology after World War II resulted in changing the color of a diamond by irradiation. The natural color of a diamond is determined by its atomic structure, which can be responsible for the absorption of light rays passing through it. When that structure is modified by the bombardment of neutrons in a cyclotron or atomic pile, the absorption pattern changes, and the diamond changes color. The new color is apparently permanent, because the earliest stones that were treated still retain their colors. Treated diamonds are not radioactive; the radiation emanating from them is less than that from a watch with phosphorescent hands and numerals.

Although any diamond can be given a new color by irradiation, this treatment is usually given only to off-white stones toward the bottom of the color scale because they can be more valuable as good yellows or greens, for examples, than lesser quality whites. A treated diamond can be as beautiful as a natural diamond of the same color, but it will not command the same price. Furthermore, it will always be identified as a treated diamond when offered for sale.

17. How do "mood rings" work?

The stone in a mood ring is often colorless quartz cemented over a capsule of liquid crystals. Liquid crystals, activated at certain temperatures, reflect light and color. When used for medical purposes, liquid crystals are painted on the skin to identify areas of different skin temperatures by their color changes.

Makers claim that these rings change color as the wearer's mood changes. According to many doctors, emotional changes can cause changes in skin temperature—especially in the hands and feet. Stored in the refrigerator for a few minutes, a mood ring stone turns black.

Index